Alexander Hunter

New National Theater Washington

D.C. A Record of Fifty Years

Alexander Hunter

New National Theater Washington
D.C. A Record of Fifty Years

ISBN/EAN: 9783743395787

Manufactured in Europe, USA, Canada, Australia, Japa

Cover: Foto ©Thomas Meinert / pixelio.de

Manufactured and distributed by brebook publishing software (www.brebook.com)

Alexander Hunter

New National Theater Washington

WASHINGTON, D. C.

A RECORD OF FIFTY YEARS

BY

Alexander Hunter.

Illustrated by J. Ellsworth Clark.

WASHINGTON, D. C.
R. O. POLKINHORN & SON, PRINTERS,
1885.

INTRODUCTION.

In a work of this character, primarily intended for information and entertainment, it is obvious that elaborate criticisms on the subjects presented in its pages would be inappropriate.

In preparing the work, we have not attempted to make it a vehicle for the expression of personal views, but as far as was consistent with the nature of the case, have confined ourselves to the historical relation of facts without assuming the function of advocate or judge. In instances which seemed to demand a verdict, we have endeavored to present illustrations of evidence rather than exhibitions of argument.

We would be ungrateful if we failed in this connection to mention the kindness of our friends in preparing these pages. The introductory chapter on early theaters is from the pen of Dr. Frank T. Howe, of this city, as is also much other interesting matter. To the untiring labor of Major Alexander Hunter, the credit of the entire work practically belongs. In season and out, he labored assiduously, always willing to render all the assistance in his power. The illustrations by Mr. J. Ellsworth Clark have been secured under great difficulty. They were taken as the building progressed, and the length of time required to photo-engrave necessarily restricted him in the number selected. To Mr. E. T. McNerhany, are we also indebted for valuable assistance.

J. H. P.

THE NATIONAL CAPITAL.

EARLY PLACES OF AMUSEMENT.

CHAPTER I.

The Washington of to-day is a city of which its people and, in fact, the whole nation is justly proud. Its broad streets and avenues are covered with asphalt pavement, smooth as a floor and easily kept clean; its sidewalks are bordered with trees and fringed with verdant parking; its public buildings have multiplied and been enlarged; and numerous statues presenting in monumental brass the heroes of our country's history adorn its various squares and parks.

The population of the city is fast approaching a quarter of a million, and the character and standing of the new comers make them desirable acquisitions. Elegant private residences and imposing business houses adorn its thoroughfares, while the great number of medium-sized dwellings testify to the comfortable and prosperous condition of the mass of its citizens.

With all this material prosperity of the city has come a corresponding intellectual development of the people. Our public school system is second to none in the country; our colleges and private educational institutions take the highest rank; our museums afford the most ample opportunity for the studies and investigations of scientists, while the Corcoran Art Gallery gives an incentive to the youthful artist by presenting for his emulation the works of the masters in painting and sculpture; our musical knowledge is more generally diffused and of a higher standard than that of any city of its size in the Union, and many of our amateur endeavors in this respect compare favorably with the representations of professional artists; our taste for the drama is of the highest order and the stamp of approval of a Washington audience is coming to be regarded as requisite to the success of a new star or a new play.

All this refinement and culture this elevated taste and critical judgment has been the growth of nearly a century. It is eighty-five years since Washington was taken possession of as the Capital of the United States and in that early period it gave little promise of its present beautiful appearance and intelligent population.

When Maj. L. Enfant, whose advent is chronicled in the Georgetown Weekly Record in the year 1794, where he is called a "distinguished astronomer," commenced his work of laying out the capital city, he had but little to encourage him save his enthusiastic belief in the future of the young Republic, and the same is probably true of Maj. Ellicott, whom the journal above quoted also styled "a distinguished astronomer;" when he started to lay out the ten miles square of territory, which was to constitute the future District of Columbia.

STROLLING COMEDIANS.

Yet even in those early days the people living in Georgetown were occasionally visited by bands of strolling players, who gave performances for the entertainment of the inhabitants of that ancient burg, and among the archives of that town, which has now lost its autonomy and become merged in the City of Washington, it is found that in the year 1799 there appeared in that ancient burg a company of strolling comedians, under the directorship of Archibald Marlborough Hamilton Sterling, for the purpose of giving a series of performances. It is also stated that this manager with the high sounding name petitioned the town authorities in behalf of himself and associates to remit the onerous tax that was imposed upon theatrical representations, amounting to $6 per night, and that the selectmen met and graciously consented to suspend the operation of this tax while the comedians were in town. It may well be imagined that the theatrical performances of that period were given in a very primitive manner, for there was no gas nor elaborate mechanical effects, and much of the circumstances attending the plot of the play and its development was left to the imagination of the audience. The entertainment commenced at early candle light and probably lasted the regulation length of three or four hours.

In searching for the early history of the drama in the District there was found in the possession of Mr. L. Moxley an old poster ten by twelve inches in size, which announced the last two nights of the "Old American Company," when the comedies of the "School for Scandal" and "Love a La Mode" would be presented. Mr. Moxley stated that this poster which gave the date of the performance as Nov. 16, 1786, came from the collection of theatrical programmes made by the late Peter Force, and that Mr. Force asserted that the performance took place in a theater which was located on the south side of Pennsylvania avenue between Four-and-a-Half and Sixth streets on the spot now occupied by Young's coach factory. It is probable that the performance took place in some other city, most likely Philadelphia, for Washington at that date was nothing but a wilderness.

That there was in the early days a dearth of amusements here, and that the deprivation was felt, is shown by a Chronicle of the year 1796, which refers to the barrenness of theatricals, and publishes from a London paper the announcement of the fact that a new play had been brought out at a Venitian theater with universal applause, entitled

"TWO GENTLEMEN OF VERONA,"

(altered from Shakespeare), with Sig. Buonaparte in the role of First Gentleman, and Sig. Beaulien in that of Second Gentleman, &c., with a triumphant entry into Milan, in which an archbishop danced a hornpipe. It was stated to be the intention of the company to visit London. This was the time that the great Napoleon was spreading terror throughout all Europe, and it was feared that his triumphant march would not be checked before he should make an assault upon the British capital.

Probably the first theatrical performance that took place in Washington was given in the year 1800, at the "Great Hotel," a tavern of considerable proportions, which was kept by a man named Blodgett, and was located on the ground now occupied by the General Post Office. Whether this Blodgett was the originator of the celebrated Blodgett claim, which has created such a stir in the District the past few years is not known. The plays that were presented on that occasion, or the actors who participated cannot be ascertained, but there is authentic record that the performance took place.

THE FIRST THEATER.

That the early settlers were anxious for amusements is evidenced by the fact that the first theater was erected in 1804. It was situated on the corner of Eleventh and C streets, on the site where the Theater Comique now stands. A stock company built it, and they gave it no other name than "The Theater." It lasted for several years, but was at length burned down, and was it sold to the elder Carusi in 1822, who reconstructed it, and named it the City Assembly Rooms. Here Carusi held his dancing academy, and in this hall were held many notable parties and balls, attended by the best people in the District. In 1857, after the National Theater was burned down the second time, Caursi's saloon was remodeled into a theater, and excellent performances took place there for long series of years before it became a variety hall. It was called the Washington Theater, and among the many notable engagements was one of two weeks, which took place in March, 1865, at the time of President Lincoln's second inauguration, by the Wallack and Davenport Combination, which introduced besides these distinguished actors, Miss Rose Etynge, Harry Placide and others. The first week was devoted to the new play of "How She Loves Him," with Wallack as the stuttering *Tom Vacil*, Davenport as *Capt. Gawley*, Harry Placide as *Diogens*, and Rose Etynge as *Atlanta Cruiser*. The second week was given to English Comedy and "The School for Scandal," "Honeymoon" and "Still Waters Run Deep" were presented.

The next theater built here was erected on Louisiana avenue, just east of Sixth street, and was first called "The Washington Theater" and afterwards "The American Theater." It must have been built some time early in the twenties, for there is a record of its having been greatly enlarged and improved in 1828. This theater enjoyed great popularity and success for a long series of years, as it had no opposition until the National was built, and at the opening address of the season, during which the National was completed, there was expressed a hope that the patrons of the establishment would not run after strange gods nor forsake old and tried friends for new ones. In this theater were held two inauguration balls and several balls and receptions by local military organizations. During the war it too, became a variety hall, and was known as "The Canterbury." If its mass of ruins could speak, they could tell many tales of struggling genius, of triumph and disappointment, of joy and sorrow, of success and despair.

OTHER THEATERS ERECTED.

With the American, Washington and National Theaters, the greater portion of the history of the District is closely interwoven, and yet there have been other theaters which it will not be out of place to name in this connection. On Pennsylvania avenue, between Four and-a-half and Sixth streets, the locality referred to by Mr. Moxley as having been designated by the late Peter Force, as the one when the 1786 performance had taken place, there was a theater called "The Adelphi," which, however, was not erected until after the building of the three principal theaters mentioned. It enjoyed several years of prosperity, however, but succeeded to its more popular rival, the National. It was destroyed by fire in 1860.

Ford's Tenth-street theater is well remembered by those in middle life, as well for the enjoyable performances that were witnessed there, as for the tragic event which forever closed its doors as a place of amusement. The original building was a Baptist church, in which the late Rev. Obediah Brown used to preach, and was altered into a theater in 1858, after the National had been burned the second time. After a brief existence of only about a year, this new theater was destroyed by fire, and the goodygood people said it was a judgment against those who had turned a house of worship into a play-house. It was rebuilt, however, and had a prosperous career during the war, until the enactment within its walls of the most tragic episode in our National history, viz.: the assassination of President Lincoln by John Wilkls Booth.

Then there was the Oxford, which was erected on the site on which Ford's Opera House now stands, and run an active competition with the Canterbury in the variety line. Mr. Wm. L.

Wall then purchased the property, and remodeled the building, which was for many years known as Wall's Opera House, and was the scene of many notable performances. Laura Keene, J. W. Wallack, Jr. and Edwin Forrest gave their last representations in this city on the stage of this Opera House, while its curtain was rung down on the death scene of poor Helen Western, who expired the following day at the Kirkwood House, a hotel which stood on the site of the present Shepherd building, at the corner of Twelfth street and Pennsylvania avenue. Fire seemed to have an especial fondness for the theaters here, for this Opera House was also burned, and on its being rebuilt was re-christened Ford's, taking the name of its lessee.

PUBLIC HALLS IN THE DISTRICT.

The Iron Hall, as it was once called, was the hall over the store now occupied by Mr. Edward Droop, No. 925 Pennsylvania avenue, and is at present utilized as a photograph establishment. In ante-bellum days many excellent performances took place here and it was on the boards of this hall that Mr. Stuart Robson made his first ambitious attempts, which by the way were lamentable failures. The hall was altered by the late W. G Metzerott, and was a favorite resort for concert troupes, magicians, &c. The gifted Parepa sang for the first time in Washington in Metzerott Hall as did also Mrs. Seguin, or Zelda Harrison as she then was. Heller, the elder Hermann and other professors of the black art, drew large crowds at this hall. During the days of the Territorial Government it was occupied by the legislative assembly and after the experiences of its feather duster heroes, the old hall was turned over to business, and has since been occupied by various photographers.

Forrest Hall in Georgetown is one of the old land marks of that older city. The date of its birth is lost in the obscurity of the dim past, and it is by no means certain that the strolling players of the last century did not make this their stopping place. It has probably seen within its walls every class of entertainment from a glove set-to up to a Shaksperean representation, and about its history cluster many interesting reminisances.

There were two Odd Fellows' Halls, one on 7th street between D and E streets, and the other on 8th street east or Navy Yard as it was then called. This latter hall was for many years occasionally visited by dramatic and musical organizations who were gladly welcomed and eagerly patronized by the Capital Hillians, for in the days before the horse-cars it was quite a journey to come up into the city The hall on 7th street was for a long while the principal hall in the city for the holding of concerts, school exhibitions and light entertainments and dramatic representations were accasionally given there. It was the home of the negro minstrel, and many a distinguished knight of the burnt cork, made his first bow to a Washington audience behind the foot-lights of Odd Fellows Hall.

Willard's Hall on F street, in the rear of Willard's Hotel, has a pleasant history dating back for several years. It was there that the first regular course of lectures was ever given in this city, and that was in 1864, and was inquired by an association, know as the Washington Lyceum composed of War Department clerks. During this season E. P. Whipple, P. T. Barnum, George Vandenhoff, the elder, and other well known lecturers appeared. The pianist Gottschalk gave his last concert in this city at Williard's Hall, being assisted by Mad. Varrien, Ed. Hoffman and Carlo Patti, the violinist, a brother of the great Adalina.

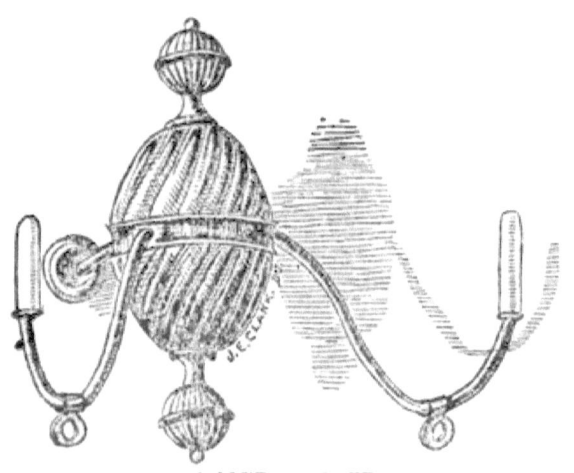

GALLERY GAS-JET.

The other halls of the district are comparativly of recent date, though their history so far as the original intention in their construction is completed. Carroll, Lincoln, Seaton and Metropolitan Halls are things of the past. The most notable event in the life of the first, was the readings of Chas. Dickens during the last visit to this city. Lincoln Hall, where Christine Nilsson made her first appearance in the National Capital, is now an Opera House at cheap prices. Seaton Hall has been turned into a billiard saloon, and the Metropolitan Hall has been promoted to a Dime Museum. The Masonic Temple and Congregational Church still fulfil the intentions of their projectors.

MODEL HOUSE OF THE DRAMA.

This sketch has been written with a desire to place in one brief record all the various places of amusement that have been erected in the District, during its life of over three-quarters of a century. Improvements have been very great in architectural style, and in all the interior appointments, both of auditorium and stage since the first theater was erected in 1804, and the handsome Opera House built last year by the Washington Light Infantry Corps, is a fine sample of the modern home of the drama. Now, however, the sixth edition of the National Theater, for this is the sixth theater that has been erected on this site, is presented to the people of the city of Washington in the form of a building in which the very latest improvements in every department have been utilized. Its awkward appearance is severely plain, but it gives the impression of massiveness and solidity. Within nothing has been omitted which could contribute in any degree to the comfort or convenience of its patrons while the decorations and ornamentation bear evidence of refined taste and skilled workmanship. The stage is spacious and is fully equipped with all the latest appliances for scenic and mechanical effects. In fact it is believed to be a Model Theater in every respect.

The National Theater has already enjoyed an existence of half a century and it is for the purpose of grouping the most notable events in its career of fifty years that the following data has been obtained after much diligent and extensive research. The incidents are arranged in chronological order, and will be found to record not only the progress and developement of the drama in the District during that period, but also to present interesting phases in the lives of many of the greatest lights in the theatrical firmament who have now gone "to that bourne from whence no traveller returns."

THE NEW NATIONAL THEATER.

WASHINGTON IN 1835.

Fifty years ago the Nation's Capital was the most ill-conditioned city on the continent. A city of magnificent distances, whose broad avenues were laid out, but not builded upon, the streets unpaved and full of huge holes and hog wallows, and the pavements in the worst possible condition. Pennsylvania avenue was in the winter and spring a vast quagmire through which vehicles toiled with extreme difficulty; slush was king, and mud monarch.

On either side of this thoroughfare were, at irregular intervals, houses of all kinds, sizes and materials—many of them being frame in the last stages of dilapidation.

Washington was then a dead city, with no trade, and kept alive only by the money of the Government employees.

Charles Dickens, in his American notes, writing up the town as late as 1842, says:

Here is Washington, fresh in my mind and under my eye. Take the worst part of the straggling outskirts of Paris, where the houses are the smallest, preserving all the oddities, especially the small shops and dwellings—burn the whole down—build it up again in wood and plaster, widen it a little, throw in a part of St. John's Wood, put green blinds outside all the private houses, with a red curtain and a white one in every window, plough up the roads, erect three handsome buildings in stone and marble anywhere, but more entirely out of everybody's way the better, call one the Post Office, one the Patent Office, and one the Treasury. Make it scorching hot in the morning, and freezing cold in the evening, with an occasional tornado of wind and dust, leave a brickfield in all central places, where a street may be naturally expected, and that's Washington.

The town boasted of no theaters worthy of the name, though there were several places of amusement. The city was small and straggling, and full houses could not be hoped for except during the sittings of Congress.

Yet every one acknowledged that the Capital of the United States ought to have a theater worthy of the name, and several patriotic citizens of the city met together and determined to form a stock company, raise funds, and erect a handsome edifice. The agitation of the new theater project culminated in a meeting held Sept. 17, 1834, when stock was subscribed for the enterprise, an association was formed, and Messrs. Henry Randall, Richard Smith, Pornelius McLean, jr., George Gibson, and William Brent were appointed a board of managers to select and purchase a lot of ground and erect suitable buildings for the purpose. These gentlemen occupied some little time in looking at sites which were offered, but finally determined upon lots 3 and 4, in square 254, which were purchased by them from John Mason, the deed bearing date of Oct. 16, 1834, and reciting the object for which the land was bought, viz, the erection and maintaining of a theater. It seems that some of those who were enthusiastic at the outset of the project failed to come to time with their subscriptions, and as the building progressed more money was needed, so on July 6, 1835, a deed was made by the managers to W. W. Corcoran, who had advised the selection of the site agreed upon, and on the following day Mr. Corcoran reconveyed the property to the trustees who were then Messrs. Henry Randall, William L. Brent, Richard Smith, and B. O. Tayloe.

THE SITE CHOSEN.

The spot was chosen, after a thorough examination and research, where the present stately building now stands. There was much difference of opinion among the stockholders before a conclusion was reached. The bulk of the city proper was grouped around the Capitol, and the buildings grew fewer and smaller as they approached the White House, hence a minority of the stockholders strongly urged the building of the theater as near the center of population as possible, and chose Capitol Hill, but the majority of the capitalists, led by the venerable W. W. Corcoran, Esq., saw with a prophetic eye that the tide of wealth and fashion must sooner or later concentrate around the President's mansion, and, so reasoning, they determined to lay the corner stone of the new temple on the place selected by Mr. Corcoran, being the same that the New National, just finished, occupies. Their judgment was vindicated by time, but not in their time; yet they builded for posterity better than they knew.

WHY IT WAS NAMED THE NATIONAL.

In the fall of 1835 the spacious edifice was completed, and at a meeting of stockholders on November 3d, the subject of a fitting

HISTORY OF THE NEW NATIONAL THEATER. 13

name was broached, and the members invited to propose a title. After each one had made his speech and submitted his choice, the committee unanimously decided to call this virgin theater the *National*. The name was typical. It was to be a house of entertainment, not so much for its own clannish citizens, as for the representatives of the whole Union; therefore, when the corner stone was laid it had that appropriate American word carved on its granite.

THE FIRST ADVERTISEMENT.

The first notice concerning the National that ever appeared in print was an offer of $50 for the best original poetical address to be spoken on the opening night. Many competed, but the prize was awarded to a Mr. Vose, of Baltimore.

The following description of the building is taken from the *National Intelligencer:*

A DESCRIPTION OF THE NEW THEATER.

The lovers of the drama will be pleased to learn that this new and beautiful theater will certainly open on Monday next. The lessees (Messrs Maywood, Rowbotham and Pratt, the proprietors of the Chestnut St. Theater, Philadelphia), have made the necessary arrangements for this purpose. The construction of the theater is admirable, both for its commodiousness and for seeing and hearing. The arrangements of the seats are very convenient, and the decorations will be elegant in every respect. The dome of the theatre is finished, and is a most beautiful thing of its kind, and when the house is lighted up the effect will be exceedingly brilliant. It is painted of a pale cerulean blue color, and is divided into four allegorical designs.

The first represents the Genius of the Institutions of the country, designated by Power and Wisdom repelling Tyranny and Superstition. The second represents Truth at the Altar, from which the Spirits of War and Peace have taken the Sword and Torch. The third represents the Goddess of Wisdom presenting a medallion of Washington to the Genius of Liberty, who returns a wreath to crown her favorite son. Fame proclaiming Victory and Peace. The last represents Justice protecting and guiding the Commerce and Manufactures of America.

The artist is a Mr. White, from New York. It will add to the public gratification when it is discovered that the whole of the ornaments of the interior are of a national character, representing either by allegorical designs or historical illustrations important events in the history of the country; this is as it should be in a NATIONAL THEATER. The painting of the principal scenery is entrusted to Mr. Kerr. In consequence of the new plan of fitting up the theatre, it is advisable to observe that the pit is done away with and the space occupied by what is termed a "parquet," which is connected with the lower boxes, and so fitted up that it will be equally desirable for the ladies to frequent as the lower boxes. The entrance and the price to the parquet and first tier of boxes will be the same, as the convenience and the gratification of the ladies have been consulted on this occasion.

The second tier of boxes will be fitted up quite as handsomely as the lower tier, and will be equally as commodious; but to meet the wishes of the citizens generally, and the constant play-goers, the price of admission will be considerably less. This tier of boxes will have the advantage of a handsome saloon being attached to it, where coffee, fruit and confectionery will be served. The gods will be pleased to see that their comforts have been duly attended to, and they will find very convenient and excellent quarters in the usual place at the usual prices.

THE FIRST PROGRAMME.
NEW NATIONAL THEATER

MAYWOOD, ROWBOTHAM & PRATT...................Lessees and Managers.
(Also of the Chestnut Street Theatre, Philadelphia.)
J. G. PRATT..Business Manager.

ENGAGEMENT OF THE LONDON AND EDINBURGH DRAMATIC COMPANY.

This Evening, December 7, 1835, will be presented the following Prologue and Prize Address by MRS. HUGHES, and Nacklen's Celebrated Comedy of

THE MAN OF THE WORLD.

Sir Pertinax Macsycophant...Mr. Maywood
Egerton, (from the London and Philadelphia Theaters)...........Mr. Cline
Lord Lumbercourt..Mr. Jefferson
Lidney, (his first appearance here)................................Mr. Senior
Melville, (his first appearance here).............................Mr. Taylor
Counsellor Plausible, (from the Chestnut Street Theater)......Mr. Eberle
Sergeant Eithside..Mr. Knight
Sam, (first appearance here).....................................Mr. Thompson
John, (first appearance here)....................................Mr. Caldwell
Tompkins, (first appearance here)...............................Mr. Weston
Lady Rodolpha Lumbercourt....................................... Mrs. Hughes
Lady Macsycophant, (her first appearance here).................Mrs. Burke
Constantia...Mrs. Knight
Betty Flint...Mrs. Jefferson
Nanny...Mrs. Baugges

The entertainment to conclude with the **Musical Farce**

TURN OUT.

Restive, (from the Chestnut Street Theater) ....Mr. Jones
Captain Summerville...Mr. Taylor
(In which he will sing "The Soldier's Tear," and "Wil't Thou Meet Me There, Love.")
Gregory..Mr. Eberle
Dr. Truckle...Mr. Jefferson
Forage...Mr. Knight
Cook..Mr. Caldwell
Gardener..Mr. Thompson
Boy..Master Burke
Marian Ramsey..Mrs. Jefferson
(In which she will sing "I am Marian Ramsey.")
Peggy..Mrs. Burke

Prices of admission: First tier of Boxes and Parquet, $1.00; second tier, 50 cents; third tier, 50 cents; gallery, 25 cents; gallery for people of color, 25 cents. Doors to be opened at a quarter past six, and performance to commence at seven o'clock precisely. Checks not transferable.

OPINION OF THE PRESS.

The opening night was a great success, and encouraged the stockholders with strong hopes that their money had been well invested. The following notice of the opening appeared in the morning paper:

The new and magnificent establishment was finely patronized on Monday evening, December 7th, 1835, by a very full house. The parquet and boxes were filled with ladies and gentlemen, and the "tout ensemble" must have formed a highly gratifying "coup d'oeil" to the spirited manager, precursor, it is hoped, of what he may expect throughout the season, providing he realizes the assurance and promises which he has made. The form of the first tier of boxes is embellished with slight sketches in imitation of bas-relief, and surrounded by correspondent ornaments representing brilliant events in maritime history, discovery, and naval achievements. The second tier of boxes is ornamented in a similar style, referring to victories, treaties, agriculture, &c. The procenium shows the same colors and style of ornaments. In the arch thereof is a representation of the Declaration of Independence, supported on the wings of Time. The curtain displays an equestrian statue of Washington, in front of rich drapery, which is partly drawn aside and displays the tomb of Washington, Mount Vernon, &c. It is intended as a substitute for the green curtain, and the change will doubtless be approved of. The machinery and stage arrangements, all excellent of their kind, are by Mr. Varden; and the whole was lighted by new and splendid lamps made expressly for this establishment.

The first star appearing in the new theater was Miss Emma Wheatley, a native born actress, of whom the papers spoke of in glowing terms of praise.

JUNIUS BRUTUS BOOTH.

The New National had a rousing audience when Junius Brutus Booth made his bow to a Washington audience as "Hamlet." Mr. Booth was the living exemplification of the axiom that "the greatest actor is the one who is the most perfect master of all the signs of the inner states of man, and could, in his own person, exhibit these signs with the most vivid power." In person Mr. Booth was short, spare, muscular, with a head and face of antique beauty, pale, but healthy pallor.

His "Iago" was the finest ever seen before the footlights. He was a splendid devil, and to "Othello" he lied like truth. His magnificent voice was at will like the blast of a bugle, or as sweet as a flute. It is no wonder that his first week in Washington was a splendid ovation.

ORCHESTRA RAILING.

THE YEAR OF 1836.—MR. WARD, MANAGER.

Mr. Ward succeeded to the management of the house in December, 1836. It was during his management that the Ravel Family made their first appearance in Washington; Burton, Vandenhoff,

Hackett and Forrest also first appeared at the National when under the management of Mr. Ward.

MISS V. MONIER, MANAGERESS.

Miss V. Monier succeeded Mr. Ward as the lessee of the theater, and she was not only an actress of considerable ability, but a lady of extraordinary business attainments She made a great success of the theater. She billed all the European and native talent, and managed the theater with wonderful ability, She was accorded a benefit at the end of each season, and was a pet and favorite with the Washingtonians.

MADAME CELESTE.

March 9, 1836, Madame Celeste gave the lovers of the melodrama a wild roving play called "The French Spy; or, the Arab of the Desert."

The gallery gods were in the seventh heaven of delight when Madame Celeste gave them "The Death Plank; or, the Wizzard's Skiff," and the "Tongueless Pirate Boy." The sentimental young ladies wept over the pathetic drama "The Moorish Page, or, The Knight of the Bleeding Scarf." The blood and thunder plays, with lurid lightning and tremulo fiddle accompaniments, must have been the rage at that time, judging from the frequency with which they were placed on the stage.

THE YEAR OF 1837.

For several months Miss Monier's Stock Company filled the boards with different plays, many of the sensational kind, that were always followed by a farce, a favorite play being Cooper's novel dramatization called the "Wept of the Wish-Ton-Wish."

GEORGE WASHINGTON PARKE CUSTIS,

the proprietor of Arlington, wrote a play called "Pocahontas," which was produced at the National, under his personal supervision, in the year 1837, and had a very successful run.

A short time after the production of "Pocahontas," Gen. Alexander Macomb, then commanding the armies of the United States, desirous of adding to his military laurels those of a dramatist, and inspired by the success attending the effort of Mr. Custis, also wrote an Indian play called "Pontiac; or, the Siege of Detroit," and this was also produced at the National, the United States marine corps being utilized in the production.

Of those who witnessed the performance a few still survive, and they describe it as a lurid and bewildering display of rapidly shifting scenes, volleys of musketry, heaps of slain Indians, &c.

THE YEAR OF 1838

The season of 1838, Mr. Junius Brutus Booth played the initial night as "Richard III.," followed by Mr. William Burton in the "Fine Old English Gentleman."

MR. WARD, MANAGER.

At the beginning of this year Miss Monier yielded up the charge of the New National, and was given a glorious send-off in the way of a farewell benefit. She went to Europe on a starring tour, and in a couple of years returned and again took charge of the theater, Mr. Ward acting as manager in her absence.

An unique entertainment must have been witnessed when Mr. Porter, the Kentucky giant, eight feet seven inches in height, and Major Stevens, a dwarf forty inches high, played in a drama together, written expressly for them, entitled "Lilliputians in Kentucky."

J. H. HACKETT.

On Thursday, May 3, 1838, the unrivalled Hackett made his bow in the New National as "Falstaff." There have been scores of Hamlets, Richards, Macbeths and Othellos, but never but one "Falstaff," and Hackett was the fat rascal personified. If the immortal bard could have seen this great comedian play "Falstaff," he would have said: "What I created in fancy, Hackett portrays in the flesh."

THE YEAR OF 1839.—EDWIN FORREST.

The dramatic year of 1839 was ushered in by Edwin Forrest.

Forrest began his dramatic career when a mere stripling. He was a conscientious, hard working student, and never neglected the smallest detail. In person he was like a Roman gladiator. His voice was absolute perfection, its crushing gutturality being supplemented with that Italian quality of transparent, round, elastic, ringing precision, which delivers the words on the silent air like crystal balls on black velvet. His Jack Cade was a splendid exhibition of physical brute power. His Claude Melnotte was as tender as a poet's wooing. He was a true actor, and sometimes when in radiant spirits he would sit on the floor, mimic a tailor at work, and convulse his friends with merriment by representing a double part of two negro wood sawyers who undertook to play Damon and Pythias. He used often to say: "Its often the case that we solemn tragedians off the stage are the jolliest dogs, while you clowns and comedians are dyspeptic and melancholy in private."

MISS ELLEN TREE.

During this year, Miss Ellen Tree, played her Shakspearean characters. She was highly spoken of. Mr. George Vandenhoff, the elder, an eminent tragedian, also trod the boards in the heavy roles.

THE YEAR OF 1840.—WARD AND WILSON, MANAGERS.

In the year 1840, Ward and Wilson, managers, received a benefit; and the season was opened at the National by little Miss Davenport, aged 11 years, from Drury Lane Theater, London, who played Richard the Third—innocence apeing villainy, a young maiden lisping like a Satyr. This precocious child filled the theater nightly during her engagement.

FANNY ELSSLER.

On Monday, July 6, 1840, the city was electrified by that graceful goddess, Fanny Elssler, the most famous danseuse on the globe. She literally turned the heads of her audience by the loveliness of her undraped limbs, and magnetized them by her exquisite poetry of motion; the audience seemed to have been changed by her Circean power into shouting lunatics, and the New National Theater was the scene of wild and extravagant action—men and women vied with each other in cheering, gentlemen hurled their watch chains and rings on the stage, and the fair sex stripped their arms of their bracelets and followed suit, until the stage floor gleamed with jewels at the feet of the adorable Elssler, who stood a veritable Danæ in this shower of gold.

THE YEAR OF 1841.—MISS V. MONIER, MANAGERESS.

In the year 1841, Miss Monier returned from her starring tour, and was received most warmly by her friends. She resumed charge of the National Theater, whose prosperity seemed to wane as soon as she left it.

BOOTH AND FORREST.

Booth and Forest played alternate weeks during the Christmas holidays.

Mr. J. W. Wallack, Herr Cline, M'lle Jasistro, and Mr. Llewellen played during the winter and spring, and the season was closed by a benefit to the National's fair manageress, Miss Monier, with " Money," its first production in Washington, and the farce of " Wives as They Were, and Maids as They Are." Miss Monier severed her connection finally with the New National Theater, and good luck and happy fortune seemed to have gone with her.

THE YEAR OF 1842—MR. WARD, MANAGER.

Mr. Ward succeeded her, and opened the season of 1842, with " Damon and Pythias," Mr. A. Adams as star. The next engagement was of three nights of Mr. Hill the delineator of Yankee character.

March 16, Miss Reynolds had a benefit, and announced that in addition to the play of "The Dead Shot," that Mr. Charles Dickens and wife would, on the occasion, honor the theater with their presence.

Next followed Signor Henrico Nano, in the startling named drama, the "Baboon; or, Rival Apes." What they were rivals for, and whether like the old song—"the baboon kissed the monkey's sister"—the play bills don't inform us.

The season was closed with a benefit to Mr. Lennox, a stock actor.

THE YEAR OF 1843.—HIELD AND TUTHILL, MANAGERS.

Season of 1843. The New National Theater was opened by Messrs. Hield and Tuthill, managers; the play was the "Stranger," with Mr. Hield in the title role. After New Year Monsieur Paul, the modern Hercules, gave a series of exhibitions of strength, among which was to let four horses be hitched to him, and try and pull him from a post.

Miss Palmer and Mr. Sinclair absolutely emptied the house, by their lugubrious acting of that dismal drama "The Stranger." They came for a week's engagement, and in two nights they closed the theater; their baggage was seized by the hotel keeper, and they issued a pitiful appeal to the charitable to help them out. A communication in the city newspapers, says they ought to be thankful to escape with their lives, after murdering the king's English as they did.

THE YEAR OF 1844.

The incoming year of 1844, was inaugurated by Mr. Hackett, whose head must have been turned by the success he met with as "Falstaff," for he came out in a proclamation, several columns in length, and announced that he would take the part of "King Richard the Third." So far so well; but when he decried Mr. Edmund Keene's rendition of the hunchbacked Gloster, as being erroneous and untrue, and intimated that he, Hackett, has the intuitive perception of the part, he placed himself in an ambiguous position, for ridicule is never so unsparing as when aimed at him who vaunts his superiority, and fails.

The card of Mr. Hackett's may have filled the old National from pit to dome on the night of January 4, 1844; but it is safe to say Hackett proved to the people that a fine comedian is not necessarily a great tragedian. His Richard lasted one night, and Falstaff disappears from the scene of his triumphs for a long time. The evening after, on the 5th of January, Mr. Booth played "Iago," and it must have been a contrast between the born tragic actor, and the aspiring Hackett, whose forte was to make tears of laughter roll down one's cheek, and not those of grief.

Tuesday, January 24, 1844. Mr. Ward, the manager, has a farewell benefit. The play is described as an entirely original one, called "Jack Nonpariel," with the inimitable Burton in the title role. The manager in his card says:

> Mr. Ward presents his compliments to the Washington public, and in announcing his farewell benefit, trusts the efforts he has made to entertain them will be remembered in his favor. He hopes that the stockholders will buy tickets and not enter upon their passes, ditto the press, in fact the free list will positively be suspended. In conclusion, Mr. Ward respectfully solicits, 'one and all' to flock to the Theater and give him a " bumper at parting."

About this time the stockholders of the old National became frightened. The shares were not salable, and the receipts were not large enough to pay the expenses, let alone a high rate of interest. Mr. Ward's retirement, after seven years hard fight against fate, brought affairs to a crisis and the stockholders hastened to get rid of their shares at a sacrifice, and the National Theater which cost $45,000 in its erection was reported sold for $13,500, to General Van Ness, Hon. Ben. Ogle Tayloe, and Mr. Richard Smith, all well known citizens of Washington.

MR. HIELD, MANAGER.

The Theater was re-opened February 11, 1844, under the management of Mr. Hield, who informs the public that the house has been thoroughly scrubbed and cleaned, the front of the Theater newly painted; extra stoves placed all through the house, and many new lamps added, so that there will be no more gloom.

The attraction on the opening night was Miss Hildreth as Julia, in the "Hunchback." This lady is the one whom Gen. Butler, then a young lawyer, became enamored, while she was in Cincinnati and subsequently married her, when she retired from the stage.

The manager soon got sick of his contract, for within three weeks he announced his farewell benefit; and on Monday, March 6, 1844, the event took place—the play being "Douglas." The Hields seemed to be a dramatic family, for the manager took the part of Glenalcon; his wife the role of

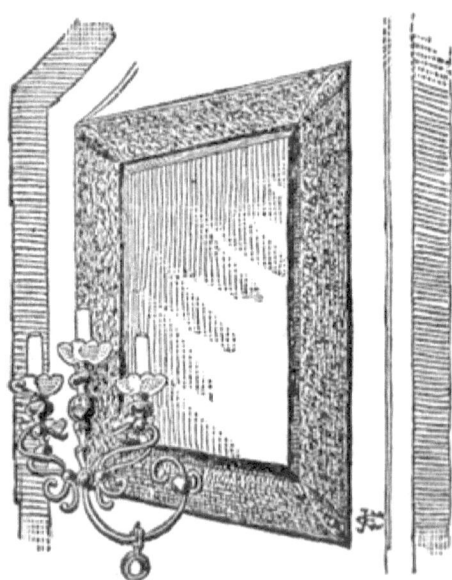

ORCHESTRA MIRROR AND GAS-JET.

Lady Randolph, and their son, "the infant phenomenon," Young Norval, that "tended his flocks on the Grampian Hills."

S. M. EMERY, MANAGER.—J. W. VANDENHOFF.

The Theater was closed for ten months. In the meantime Mr. S. M. Emery, of the Holliday Street Theater, Baltimore, became the lessee, and Mr. Vandenhoff, of Covent Garden, London, was the attraction, as "Hamlet." Mr. Vandenhoff was followed by the Italian Opera Troupe from Havana, with Signora Corsini, soprano, and Signor Perrozi, tenor, as the stars.

OLE BULL.

On Christmas night, 1844, the Theater was jammed with a brilliant audience to welcome Ole Bull, who played only two nights—the price of admission being raised to one dollar. The house was then closed and an army of workmen were busy all Christmas week in transforming the Theater into a circus, and making the pit and stage a spacious amphitheatre. On January 4, 1844, N. A. Howes' Equestrian Troupe performed, and the clown cracked the same old jokes that were dug up at Ninevah and Pompeii.

The manager, Mr Emery, went the way of his predecessors, and farewelled out of Washington, from which frequent changes, we conclude that running a theater in the National Capital in those days was what Mr. Mantalini would call a "demnition risky business."

THE YEAR OF 1845.—WM. E. BURTON, MANAGER.

On January 10, 1845, Mr. W. E. Burton, lessee of the Philadelphia and Baltimore theaters, announces that he has leased the National, which he has repainted and re-decorated, and will open on January 12, with a stock company, Mr. Anderson as the star. This engagement appeared to languish. The company played before a beggarly array of empty benches, the people either did not go, or there was bad management somewhere. The following communication, that appeared in the *Intelligencer*, may give a hint where the trouble was. If the fashion and wealth of the city were not theater goers, the roughs and street arabs evidently were steady patrons and paid their money, got their tickets and went in for an evening enjoyment, in their own way.

"An old sitter" hits at the abuses, in a style that Artemus Ward would call "sarkasum," and as a sign of the times we publish it entire:

THEATER REFORM.

WASHINGTON, FRIDAY, JANUARY 17, 1845.

Messrs. EDITORS:

I beg leave to submit through the columns of your paper the subjoined rules for the better management of the theater.

Vive la politeise, OLD SITTER.

1. That no spectator be expected to sit, if he chose to stand; it being a gross infringement of the rights of an American citizen to attempt to restrict or otherwise regulate the free use of his limbs.
2. That for like return, he elevate his legs, or stick them at any angle, oblique or acute, most conducive to his comfort.
3. That the good old National divertisement of chewing and spitting tobacco, ad libitum, is an inalienable right of the American citizen.
4. That on a benefit night any individual may use three seats for the accommodation of his feet, cudgel, dog or other indispensable appurtenance.
5. That no spectator, whether standing or sitting, be subjected to the impertinent cry of "hats off in front."
6. That any attempt to suppress loud talking, whooping, haw-hawing, swearing or the like, will not be tolerated, as it is a most fragrant violation of that great safeguard of the Republic, the liberty of free speech.
7. That in the event of a set to, between two belligerents, that they be allowed to have it out, undisturbed to those minions of the law, called police.
8. That for the encouragement of native musical talent the standing orchestra overture shall be some approved "chef d'œuvre," of the great Ethiopian masters, as "Possum Up the Gum Tree," "Sally Come Up," "That Yellar Gal Smiled at Me."
9. That a copy of these regulations be affixed to the play bills.

Salve Republica, OLD SITTER.

The old National, from natural and artificial causes, was not a paying success. It is most probable that the true reason why the audiences were not large arose from the fact that the city was spread over such a vast area, and the streets, all unpaved, were so hard to travel, that it required real courage and laborious work to go to the theater from any distance. There were no vehicles then save the two horse hacks, who charged ten dollars to carry a person to the theater and bring him back home, nor were there any street cars. Pennsylvania avenue was lighted by oil lamps; but the rest of the city was wrapped in Cimmerian darkness.

The National Theater was like a castle in a state of siege: there was only one route to reach it, all the other avenues of approach were closed by muddy roads, impassable swamps—treacherous quagmires—over which deep darkness brooded until morning.

For some years the theater was sometimes open, but oftener closed. A stock company played alternately in Philadelphia and in Baltimore, and as the two latter cities patronized the drama more regularly and certainly, the company of course acted where they made the most money, and at last rarely came to Washington except during the sessions of Congress.

The route system, with its mathematical arrangement of dates, and constant succession of travelling stars was not then conceived of, and the troupes generally roved at will, and remained at towns where they had the heaviest pecuniary returns.

HISTORY OF THE NEW NATIONAL THEATER. 23

The first fire took place on Wednesday night, March 5, 1845, and the advertisement of that date shows that the attractions were as follows:

The Inimitable Burletta of
BEAUTY AND THE BEAST.

Sir Aldgate Pump..Mr. W. E. Burton
John Quill...Mr. Burke
Selima...Mrs. Burke

After which THE CONGO MELODISTS will appear as refined gentlemen of the North.
After which the excellent comedietta of
THE SCAPE GOAT; OR, CUPID AND THE CLASSICS.
To conclude with a new farce, called the
STAGE-STRUCK NIGGER.

The account of the conflagration, which appeared in the *National Intelligencer*, on the following day, was as follows:

THE NATIONAL THEATER BURNT.

An unusually destructive fire occurred in this city last night, between eight and nine o'clock, which consumed the handsome edifice, erected but a few years ago, known as the National Theater, besides some seven or eight dwelling-houses, situated on the southeast corner of the same square, and fronting on Pennsylvania Avenue and Thirteenth street, in addition, we believe, to several stables and other buildings which stood in the alleys that pass through the square.

The fire originated in what is called the oil room, in the back part of the Theater, while the performances of the evening were in progress; but fortunately for the persons in attendance, who composed a very large and respectable audience of both sexes, the alarm was given sufficiently soon to allow them all to escape from the burning building without the happening of any serious accident.

The Theatre was burnt entirely out, leaving the bare walls alone standing. We believe it was lately purchased from the company who erected it, by Mr. Benjamin Ogle Taylor, of this city, whose loss must be considerable, especially, if our information be correct, that there was no insurance upon the property. Mr. Burton was the lessee, who has also, no doubt, suffered much loss. We do not know who the other sufferers are, except that our worthy fellow citizen Mr. Charles J. Nourse was one of them and Mr. Louis Vivans another.

The Globe Printing Office, which occupies the lot on the west side of the Theater, was saved from injury by being protected by the high and thick walls of the latter building, and on account of the wind blowing pretty freely at the time from the west, which carried the flames in an opposite direction.

CHAPTER II.

THE SECOND OPENING.

THE YEAR OF 1850.—WILLARD AND REESIDE, MANAGERS.

JENNY LIND.

In the year 1850, the fame of Jenny Lind was on everybody's tongue; with her divine voice she had the whole of Europe at her feet, and she crossed the Atlantic to subjugate the New World Of course it would not do to let her come to America without visiting its Capital, and giving her statesmen an opportunity of offering her not only a democratic but a royal welcome But there was a serious barrier to her professional appearance, there being no suitable and appropriate hall for her voice in the city. There was but one Jenny Lind in the world, and the stigma of Washington, the Capital of twenty million of people, not having a musical hall, must be removed.

Two prominent Washingtonians took the matter in hand—they were Messrs. Willard and Reeside who built a hall upon the ancient National ruins, using,

MIRROR.

the old bricks therefor. In a card to the public these gentlemen lay stress upon the fact that they employ only workmen who are natives of the city. The hall was rapidly and hurriedly built to get ready for the great artist's visit during the Christmas holidays. Anticipating the immense crowd that would jam the concert hall, the building was examined by Robert Mills, architect, and pronounced safe.

The excitement upon the night of Jenny Lind's concert surpassed anything ever witnessed in Washington. Crowds stood from midnight to nine in the morning in front of the theater watching for the box office to open, and it required all the police force to keep order. Nothing was talked of but Jenny Lind; she was the absorbing theme. The highest dignitaries called upon her, and no empress ever held a more sovereign court than did this little lady in the Republican Capital. This wonderful singer who was to enthrall and delight the music lovers that were sojourning at the Capital, was, by common consent, ranked as the greatest soprano singer that ever lived.

She was born in Stockholm in 1820. She studied under Herr Crelins, and made her debut with brilliant prospects, but when she was fifteen years old she lost her voice entirely. Several years after it slowly returned, and she then renewed her studies under Mad. Malibran.

In 1852 she married in Boston a young German pianist, Otto Goldschmidt.

Her American tour was a series of splendid triumphs, and her goodness and benevolence, rare in one so young, won the love of the American public.

With the plaster scarcely dry, and the smell of paint painfully apparent, the hall threw open its doors to the streaming crowd, that speedily filled it from top to bottom. In a few minutes there was not standing room.

The following is a copy of the play bill:

NEW NATIONAL HALL.

WILLARD & REESIDE .... Proprietors.
JAS. E. WELSH .... Business Manager.

GRAND OPENING NIGHT OF THE NEW NATIONAL HALL.

Engagement of the World-Renowned
MADEMOISELLE JENNY LIND,
Supported by a Strong Company. This evening, Monday, Dec. 16th, 1850.

PROGRAMME.
PART I.
Conductor .... Mr. Benedict
Overture—Zampa .... Harold
Scena and Aria—Sorgette .... Marometto
Secundo—Signor Belletti .... Rossini
Scena and Aria—Casta Diva .... Norma
    (Mademoiselle Jenny Lind.)
Thiede—Caprici de tremolo—solo violin .... De Berriott
    (Mr. Joseph Burke.)
Trio for voice and two flutes .... Camp of Silesia
   (Composed expressly for Mlle. Lind's voice by Myenberger.)
Voice .... Mlle. Lind
Flutes .... Messrs. Kyle and Siede

PART II.
Overture—Crown of Diamonds .... Auber
Barcarola—Sella poppa del mio brick—Sig. Belletti .... Ricci
Grand March—Crusaders .... Benedict
The Bird Song—Mlle. Jenny Lind .... Taubert
The Tarrantula—Sig. Belletti .... Rosini
Greeting to America, Prize song, written by .... Bayard Taylor
    (Mlle. Jenny Lind.)
The Herdman Echo Song .... Mlle. Jenny Lind

PRICES OF ADMISSION.
Secured Seats close to the Stage $7 00
   "   "   middle of Hall 5 00
   "   "   Back 4 00
Doors open at 6 p. m., Concert to commence at 8 p. m.
No Checks issued.

The *Intelligencer* the next morning had the following:

> Mlle. Jenny Lind's concert last night was attended by the largest, most brilliant, and certainly the most gratified audience which ever assembled at any public entertainment in this city.
>
> We doubt if an individual in the audience had prior to her appearance an adequate idea of the enchanting melody the "dulcet and harmonious breadth" of the peerless songstress.

In the second concert, the President and Vice-President of the United States and his Cabinet, and the members of the Supreme Court attended in a body. The most extraordinary mark of homage that this country ever witnessed before or since to an artiste.

THE YEAR OF 1851.

On January 21, 1851, the National Hall was changed into a circus, and tiers upon tiers of hastily constructed seats were erected along the walls, and as the crowd was enormous the pressure was very great; during the exciting part of the programme, the west side of the wall fell outward and carried many people with it. A scene of frantic confusion ensued, that was with difficulty allayed by cooler, and calmer minds. An examination was made, and no one found badly hurt, though many were almost frightened out of their senses. After a while the performers commenced their parts, and the programme kept on until its close. This was the last performance at the National Hall. Hardly had the adorable voice of Jenny Lind, and the hoarse voice of the ring master ceased to reverberate through the building, before masons were at work tearing the whole superstructure down, and immediately the energetic managers were busy re-building the theater on a grander scale then ever before.

CHAPTER III.

THE YEAR OF 1852—E. A. MARSHALL, MANAGER.

THE THIRD OPENING.

Early in December, 1852, the National Theater was re-built for the third time, the following card announcing the fact:

WASHINGTON, D. C., December 10, 1852.

E. A. Marshall, lessee of the Broadway, New York, and Walnut Street, Philadelphia, theaters, respectfully announces to the citizens of Washington, that he has leased the National Theater, which has been re-built and re-modelled in a magnificent manner, at an enormous outlay, and is now one of the most elegant temples of the drama in the United States.

On December 15, 1852, the house was crowded—the President and his Cabinet being present to honor the occasion. Mrs. Hield, who seemed always on hand, spoke the opening address, and then the play bill tells the rest.

NEW NATIONAL THEATER.

E. A. MARSHALL..Lessee
(Also of the Broadway and Walnut Street Theater.)
W. M. FLEMING..Stage Manager
J. B. BENSIL..Treasurer

OPENING NIGHT, DECEMBER 15, 1852.

Great Attraction. Engagement of MISS MATILDA HERON, and her Unrivalled Stock Company. This evening will be presented THE HUNCHBACK, with the following cast:

JULIA..MISS MATILDA HERON
CLIFFORD..Mr. Fleming
(Characters by the rest of the Company.)

PRICES OF ADMISSION.

Private Boxes...$10 00
Parquet..75
First Circle..75
Second Gallery..25
Colored Gallery..25
Pit..50

(Gentlemen are earnestly requested to use the spittoons and spare the floor.)

The papers speak in glowing terms of the initial success, and pays the following compliment to the lessee and manager:

If the present lessee fails to make the New National Theater the most pleasant and paying institution of the city, no other man in this country can flatter himself with the expectation of success.

HISTORY OF THE NEW NATIONAL THEATER. 29

On December 22, 1852, the important announcement is made to the Washington public, that for the first time in the history of this city, they will have the opportunity of hearing the Grand Italian Opera in all of its completeness.

The troupe, with Madame Torronte, soprano, and Signor Vorrello, tenor, as stars, played only one night, giving Rossini's Opera of "Cinderella."

THE YEAR OF 1853.

In the new year of 1853, Madame Celeste opened with a fine company, and played three nights in a comedy called "Ducarge."

MISS JULIA DEAN.

The next week, January 12, Miss Julia Dean made her debut at the National, and won a dazzling success in the part of Julia in the play—Sheridan Knowles' "Hunchback." Her rendition of Julia carried the house by storm, and rarely had the Old or New National ever witnessed a greater triumph.

The following standing avertisement was kept in the morning paper:

Notice to the National Theater patrons. We are pleased to inform the public that we have made arrangements with the Union Line of Omnibusses to run between Georgetown and the theater, before and after the performance. Fare 25 cents each way.

LOLA MONTEZ.

The Washington people had a real sensation on February 9, 1853. The lovely Lola Montez, the fairest, the frailest, the most fascinating woman of modern times appeared at the theater as Theodosia, in the mournful tragedy of the "Maid of Croissy."

The fair Lola had not much histrionic ability, but she jammed the theater, and brought the ducats into the till. She was fond of late suppers, and the first men of the times gave private entertainments to her and a few select friends. She set the town on fire with her beauty, and played havoc with the masculine hearts.

The next week the original play, "Betrothed" was brought out with Mr. Couldock as the attraction, and he was followed by Miss Eliza Logan, in the tragedy of "Evadne; or, the Statue."

On March 1, 1853, one of Boucicault plays was for the first time put on the boards of the National Theater. The piece was "London Assurance," with Miss J. Bennett as Lady Gay Spanker.

The "Hunchback" must have been a favorite tragedy at that time, for it was played for the eighth time at the National, by Miss Davenport (now Mrs. Gen. Lander), her second appearance in Washington in that character.

CHARLOTTE CUSHMAN.

The gifted Miss Charlotte Cushman made her first appearance before a Washington public on April 1st. She scored a royal success in her roles of "Lady Macbeth," "Rosalind," and "Julia."

SEGUIN OPERA COMPANY.

The succeeding week, for the first time, an English Opera Company played at the National. It was called the Seguin Opera Troupe and achieved great success; their repertoire consisting of "Daughter of the Regiment," "Martha," "Il Trovatore," and the "Beggar's Opera."

They were followed by Edwin Forrest, who drew better houses than any other tragedian in the country.

The queenly Charlotte Cushman, then in the very zenith of her glory, played her farewell engagement here preparatory to her departure for Europe. Her "Ophelia" was a fine exhibition of her splendid powers. The Washington Light Infantry, and the Washington Continental Guards, attended the theater in full uniform in her honor, and as a graceful recognition of the compliment, she gave them an elegant wine supper after the performance at the National Hotel.

DRESS CIRCLE RAILING AND DECORATION.

EMMA FITZPATRICK.

Miss Cushman was followed by Miss Emma Fitzpatrick, from Drury Lane Theater, London, who made her debut December 20, 1853, as Letitia Hardy, in the "Belle's Stratagem." There was also a grand corps de ballet, with Senorita Sota as the star danseuse.

The succeeding week Anna Cora Mowat, the authoress, who had turned actress, trod the boards in "Adrienne." This lady, a short while after this engagement, married a son of "Father Ritchie," the editor of the *Union*.

The Chinese Magicians drew crowded houses by their hotch potch of farce, ledgerdemain, and gymnastics.

On the evening of April 3d, 1853, a grand complimentary benefit was tendered the popular manager, Mr. E. A. Marshall, as a tribute to his enterprise during his successful management. The theater on this occasion was crowded to its utmost capacity—the play, as it was presented, having in its cast the leading actors of his theaters in New York and Philadelphia. We present the entire bill in full, that our readers may learn how they presented plays in the "Auld Lang Syne" days before the war.

NATIONAL THEATER.

Washington, D. C.

MR. E. A. MARSHALL...SOLE LESSEE, (Also of the Broadway (N. Y.) and Walnut street (Philadelphia) Treaters.)
ACTING AND STAGE MANAGER............................... Mr. A. W. FENNO.

PRICES OF ADMISSION.

Private Boxes, $5; Dress Circle and Parquette, 50 cts., Children under ten years, half price; Reserved Seats, 75 cts.; Orchestra Seats, 75 cts.; Family Circle, 25 cts.; Third Tier, 50 cts.; Colored Gallery, 25 cts.

Doors open at 7 o'clock, Performance commences precisely at half-past 7 o'clock. The Box Office will be open daily, from 10 o'clock a. m., to 4 o'clock p. m.
Mr. H. B. MATTERSON...TREASURER.

Grand Complimentary Benefit to MR. E. A. MARSHALL.

CORRESPONDENCE, &C.

WASHINGTON, April 7, 1853.

DEAR SIR: Desiring to render you a tribute of respect for the enterprise you have manifested in presenting the citizens of Washington and vicinity, and those sojourning for a limited period here, with a series of interesting and attractive dramatic performances since you assumed the management of the National Theatre, the undersigned respectfully solicit the privilege of tendering you a Complimentary Benefit, upon such evening before the close of the present season, as you may be pleased to designate. Soliciting your acceptance of this evidence of our appreciation of your exertions we are, very respectfully, your obedient servants, John W. Forney, John L. Smith, Chubb Brothers, Henry Polkinhorn, Geo. Gibson, R. Armstrong, W. B. Chase, John F. Coyle, N. Clinch, John A. Bryant, Samuel L. Harris, P. Harry Hayes, R. B. Hackney, M. A. Dexter, F. S. Shulze, J. W. Arnold, Thos. Florence, C. Eames, H. A. Willard, W. H. Kennon, Daniel Buck, C. W. Flint, P. H Brooks, C. P. Wilhelm, Chas. W. Boteler, J. Thomas, Chas. H. Winder, Roger A. Pryor, James S. Holland, W. M. Overton, J. K. Bailey, E. W. Abbott, Clark Mills.

PHILADELPHIA, April 13, 1853.

GENTLEMEN Your favor of the 7th instant is received. I accept with high gratification your generous offer of a complimentary Benefit. To know that my exertions have won the approbation of gentlemen so distinguished by social position and intellectual attainments is an ample reward for all past labors, and will inspire me to make fresh efforts. I would suggest **Monday the 18th instant.**, as the time, if that will be agreeable to yourselves.

With grateful acknowledgemnts,

I am, gentlemen, your obedient servant,

E. A. MARSHALL.

To Col. **J. W. Forney,** Chubb Brothers, H. Polkinhorn, George Gibson, R. Armstrong and others, Washington.

On which occasion will be presented a fashionable and sterling entertainment; the whole of THE NATIONAL COMPANY and ORCHESTRA having volunteered, also MR. RICHINGS, MISS RICHINGS, MR. MCKEON, AND MRS. DUFFIELD, of the Walnut street Theatre.

On **Monday evening, April 18th,** the performance to commence with R. B. Sheridan's sterling Comedy, in 5 acts, called the

SCHOOL FOR SCANDAL,

With the following unrivalled cast:

Sir Peter Teazle..Mr. P. Kichings
Sir Oliver Surface..Cunningham
Joseph Surface...Foster
Charles Surface..Fenno
Crabtree...Jordan
Sir Benjamin Backbite......................................Wheatleigh
Rowley..McKeon
Moses...Dewalden
Trip..Tining
Snake...Mr. Terry
Careless..Day
Joseph's Servant..Francis
Eady Sneerwell's Servant..................................Haymer
Lady Teazle...Mrs. Duffield
Maria...Cunningham
Mrs. Candor...Gladstane
Lady Sneerwell..France
Maid..Terry

LA POLONAISE BY MISS ANNIE WALTERS.

To conclude with the Musical Farce, in 2 acts, of a

ROLAND FOR AN OLIVER.

Alfred **Highflyer**...Mr. P. Richings
Sir Mark **Chase**..Cunningham
Mr. Selborne..Day
Game-keepers..Haymer I. Francis
Fixture...Mrs. H. V. Jordan
Maria Darlington..Miss C. Richings
Mrs. Selborne...Mrs. Thorpe
Mrs. Fixture..France

MISS RICHINGS will sing the following songs—"MY HAPPY HOME," variations from "LES DIAMANS DE LA COURONNE," **and dance a new WALTZ** by GUSTAVE BLESNER, of Philadelphia.

On Wednesday evening next, April the 20th, PROFESSOR ANDERSON, The renowned Wizard of the North, will commence an engagement for six nights only.

No money taken at the Doors. Tickets to be purchased at the Box Office.

NOTICE.—Arrangements have been made with the UNION LINE of omnibusses to run between Georgetown and the Theatre before and after the performance. Fare 12½ cents.

An EFFICIENT POLICE will be in constant attendance to preserve strict order.

HISTORY OF THE NEW NATIONAL THEATER.

Wednesday April 20, 1853, Prof. Anderson, the great **Wizard**, showed his powers for the first time in Washington.

The theater was closed a week and then opened by Donizetti's acting dogs, monkeys, and goats. This drew the children in flocks, and all the schools gave half holiday to let the scholars attend in a mass. One afternoon Mr. Donizetti gave a matinee to the orphan asylums of the city free of charge.

THE RAVEL FAMILY.

The Ravel Family then played four consecutive weeks, and were followed by a few plays by stock performers, when the theater closed for the summer.

JULIAN CONCERTS.

The Julian Concerts awoke an extraordinary degree of enthusiasm among our people, and such a conglomeration of musical genius was rarely gathered together. The prices were greatly advanced; notwithstanding the house was packed to the very utmost limit. The *Intelligencer* said the morning after:

When the hour—half-past seven—arrived, from two to three thousand citizens were gathered in boxes and parquet. When the orchestra, led by Count Julian, played a medley of American airs, the enthusiasm of the house was raised to the highest pitch, and when the national anthem Hail Columbia was performed in a manner unequaled before, the vast audience was lifted to their feet, and the triumph recorded in three tremendous cheers.

The next week Mlle Yrca Mathias, the celebrated Russian Danseuse with her corps de ballet, drew fine houses.

THE YEAR OF 1854.

The season of 1854 was opened brilliantly by the Grand Italian Opera Company, with Rose de Vries in the leading role.

GRISI AND MARIO.

Just about this time the music loving, art enjoying public in Washington were on the tip toe of expectation, for their ears were soon to be ravished by the clearest, most passionate soprano, and the grandest tenor on earth combined—that of Grisi and Mario—who were singing together in opera; such an event in the world of music was so rare, that no one who loved the "concord of sweet tones" would willingly forego.

Gialitto Grisi was the greatest Italian dramatic singer since the days of Malibran. She made her debut in 1832, in the role of "Semiramide." The regular beauty of her features, the truth, flexibility, and compass of her voice, made her a wonderful success from the first. The great Composer Bellini wrote the opera, "Il Puritani" especially for her. She was universally quoted as a type of what the lovers of Italian opera call "passion" in a singer

Her favorite role was "Norma," and she became so identified with the part as to be often called "The Diva."

Mario's tenor voice was the most enthralling ever heard. Owen Meredith has immortalized it in verse in his "Aux Italiens."

> Of all the operas that Verdi wrote
>   The best to my taste is the "Trovatore,"
> And Mario can soothe with a tenor note
>   The souls in Purgatory.
>
> The moon in the tower slept soft and low,
>   And who has not thrilled in the strangest way
> As we heard him sing, while the gas burned low,
>   "Non il scordar di me."

For weeks their advent was talked of, and when it was known that they would only sing one night, and the opera was "Norma;" with Grisi as the Diva and Mario as Pollione, and Signor Arditi, musical director, the rush for seats was maddening; the manager was besieged in his house; the proudest statesmen of the land deigned to sue for a small spot in the theater, even to place a camp stool. The scale of prices was no bar. The lower boxes sold, for the one performance, for $75; the upper ones for $50; orchestra seats were $10; the parquet $7.50; the balcony and peanut gallery $5; probably had the manager had the conscience to have increased these stupendous prices fourfold, such was the intense desire to hear these transcendent singers, that the public would have paid the price ungrudgingly. The lucky possessors of tickets were cajoled and implored on all sides to sell. It was a common thing to buy in a ticket for one, two, or even five hundred dollars. A Virginian named Warrick, from Richmond, an old "Forty-Niner," who had just returned from the mines of California with the sale of a rich placer, and his pockets lined with "pay-rock," promised several of his friends to take them to the opera, and actually paid a member of Congress $1,000 for his private box.

The National never seemed nearer Heaven than it did on the night of January 6, 1854, when those two divine voices blended in a glorious harmony; it was simply perfection, and when the enthralled audience filed out the lighted theater into the dark night, it seemed as if they had just awoke from a seraphic dream, with the celestial supernatural melody still ringing in their ears. Of all the triumphs of art, there was no greater than this.

The great Forrest played three continuous weeks, commencing February 6. His repertoire consisted of "Hamlet," the "Gladiator," "Jack Cade," "Claude Melnotte," and "Macbeth." He was finely supported and of course, actor and manager alike, reaped a golden harvest. He was followed by Mrs. Farren in the play of "The Stranger." Then Miss Ince brought out that everlasting play, "The Hunchback," and made a most tearful Julia.

Mrs. Macready came March 20th, and drew fair audiences to witness her "Meg Merriles."

BOILER ROOM.

MISS AGNES ROBERTSON.

Pretty, piquant Agnes Robertson, who afterwards married Dion Boucicault, tripped across the stage in her dashing, charming way as Milly the "Maid with her Milking Pail," with her short skirts and neat ankles; it was worth the price of admission just to see her sparkling face.

The summer being very near, Count Julian gave three concerts, and the theater was closed until autumn.

MATILDA HERRON.

The fall season of 1854 was opened by Matilda Herron, one of the greatest emotional actresses of her time, and the pioneer in that particular line of acting. She had just returned from London and Paris where her progress was unparalleled in the European success of any American actress that had preceded her. Her role was "Camille," with Mr. W. H. Briggs of Holiday Street Theater as Armand. She met with an ovation that would have satisfied the soul of the most exacting artist.

KUNKLE AND FORD, MANAGERS.

In the meanwhile there had been an entire change of control of the National. George Kunkle became manager and John T. Ford, of the Holliday Street Theater, Baltimore, treasurer. The theater property became more valuable every year. The tide of population was steadily moving up town; the streets were well paved and the wealth of the city was congregating in its near vicinity.

Mr. James W. Wallack played one night as "Macbeth," supported by Mrs. Melinda Jones. Mr. Wallack certainly had a good advertising agent who billed him well, as the following specimen will show:

> In France the Emperor, forgetting the cares of state, and dashing the glittering show of pomp and royalty aside, was wont to go to the theater to enjoy the intellectual repast furnished by the gifted Wallack and Jones.

The manager placed on the boards, the Nightingale Troupe, as he called them; and he speaks of their musical and terpsichorean portraiture of life among the negroes of the south—we conclude they were blacked up—or, as the gallery Gods would say, the performance was "horse opera."

THE YEAR OF 1855.

In January the Rousset Sisters, with their coryphees, tripped their fantastic toes, much to the edification of the young bloods and old bachelors of the Metropolis.

J. A. KEENAN, MANAGER.

George Kunkle here retires from the management and J. A. Keenan takes his place.

A play, to please the southern audience, is now put on the stage as an offset to Harriet Beacher Stowe's creation. It is called "Uncle Tom as He is; or, True Southern Life."

J. E. MURDOCK.

On Washington's birthday, Mr. J. E. Murdoch trod the stage of the National for the first time; he appeared as "Hamlet," and, just to think of it, Mr. Joseph Jefferson, the popular comedian, will chant the dismal, doleful history of "Villekins and his Dinah," as originally sung by him with uproarious applause in Baltimore.

After Murdock comes the Patomime, for the first time, of "The Red Gnome; or, the Spirit of the Silver Fountain." The next night was "Cinderella; or, the Little Glass Slipper." The papers tell us that the children went wild over this performance. The National was then closed until autumn.

HENRY C. JARRETT, MANAGER.

Another entire change of management: this time Mr. Henry C. Jarrett, who afterwards became a famous New York manager, and who was then the owner of the Museum of Baltimore, became the lessee of the National with Mr. Joseph Jefferson as stage manager.

They opened the theater with Mr. J. R. Scott, in the poem dramatized, called "The Lady of the Lake."

The circus then became the attraction at the National, the parquette and orchestra being planked so as to allow a saw dust ring to be formed.

October 26, pretty and versatile Agnes Robertson again played to a delighted audience. Among the charms of the vaudeville is the great transformation scene of a cat changed into a woman, in which Miss Robertson, Mr. Joseph Jefferson, Mr. J. B. Howe, and Mr. Ellis appeared.

Doubtless a good many of the audience well knew, from their personal observation, that such a transformation was made oftener off the stage than on.

In October, Matilda Herron again delights and thrills the audience by the rendition of "Camille."

She was followed by a dashing Frenchwoman in the sensational play of "Jack Shepherd, the Highwayman," in four acts and forty-two tableaux. It was estimated that every boot black and street Arab in Washington witnessed this drama. They not only filled their own gallery, but overflowed into the circle, balcony and parquet; their applause was deafening. One philanthropic gentleman of Washington made the boys a present of one hundred tickets and he never had to pay for a "shine" afterwards, so long as he lived in Washington.

JOHN E. OWENS.

Mr. John E. Owens, on November 11, 1855, started off well as Dromio in the "Comedy of Errors," and played the balance of the week to fair audiences. Then Mr. and Mrs. Barney Williams stepped before the National's footlights. They played "Irish Assurance," and "Limerick Boy."

The succeeding week, Mr. J. W. Wallack gave "Macbeth," and Mr. Joe Jefferson a farce called "An Affair of Honor." Mr. and Mrs. Williams then returned and played another week.

A southern actor next came and gave the old English comedy of the "Heir at Law," and following him was Miss Eliza Logan in the dramatized "Lucretia Borgia."

E. L. DAVENPORT.

Mr. Edwin L. Davenport made his first appearance in Washington in Christmas week, in "Richard the III." Mr. Jefferson playing a farce, "Slasher and Crasher."

Succeeding him was James E. Murdoch as "Hamlet."

THE YEAR OF 1856.

The new year the National was brilliantly inaugurated by the production of "The School for Scandal," with a caste of extraordinary merit. Sir Peter **Teazle was** Mr. Henry Placide, Charles **Surface,** Mr. James E. **Murdoch**; Joseph Surface, Mr. J. W **Wallack, Jr.**; Careless, Mr. **A. H.** Davenport; **Moses,** Mr. Joseph **Jefferson**; Sir Benjamin Backbite, Mr J. M. Davidson; Snake, Mr. **Edwin Adams**; Lady Teazle, Miss Lizzie **Weston**; and Mrs. **Candour,** Miss Kate Howe. There **never were so many distinguished players ever** combined together **in a comedy, at least in Washington, and for** a week "standing **room only"** was placarded in the lobby.

MAX MARETZEK.

Max Maretzek for the first time appeared **in Washington with his Italian** Opera Troupe, with Madame de Baroness **Anna De Lagrange.** The opera "Il Trovatore" was given **two nights to** a large and **cultivated** audience.

F. S. CHANFRAU AND M'LLE ALBERTINE.

On January 16, Chanfrau and Miss Albertine played in comedy, "The First Night" and "Black Eyed Susan," being the attraction. They **were succeeded by** Mr. Roothroyd Flairclough, who portrayed the "**Moor of Venice."** On their heels came Susan and **Kate Denin, who, being ambitious, they** struck high, Miss **Susan essaying the role of the noble Dane who loved** Ophelia, **and Romeo who was beloved by the fairest of the House of the Capulets.** It is said no **woman can play "Hamlet,"** and the blue eyed Susan **was probably no exception to the rule.**

The "Naid Queen," a spectacular drama, **came next, and** it had the honor of ushering in a day performance. It seems singular that twenty **years should elapse before the custom of matinees was** inaugurated in this theater; but enterprise or reform was an innovation that **the theater was the last to yield to, and it seems a real blindness on the** part of the manager that the idea never crossed **their minds; it would** have saved many of the directors **of this theater** from their utter failure. Certainly no lessee of the present day would rent a theater if he had to do without the matinee, which is the more profitable, generally, than **any** night performance.

KUNKLE & CO., MANAGERS.

Another change of the officers is announced in March, 1856. Kunkel & Co., became the lessees, Mr. Joseph Jefferson retired, and John T. Ford came to be manager. They had the supervision of the Holiday Street Theater at Baltimore and the Marshall Theater at Richmond, Virginia, at this date.

MAGGIE MITCHELL.

They opened with Miss Maggie Mitchell, who made her first bow before the Washington public in a play called "The Little Treasure."

HISTORY OF THE NEW NATIONAL THEATER. 39

Then came in succession Miss Agnes Robertson, Pyne and Harrison's English Opera Troupe, Mr. Jas. Wallack, in the "Iron Mask;" Mr. J. H. Hackett, in "Henry IV.;" Mrs. Farren, in "Jane Shore." And the summer season ended with a benefit to the lessee, Mr. George Kunkel, in the drama of "The Washington Firemen."

The fall season was opened September 8th, by Miss Laura Keene, in "Camille."

PARODI.

Maurice Strakosh now appeared upon the scene for the first time with the famous Parodi. She studied in Paris under the tuition of Pasta, and at the close, Pasta embraced her pupil and addressed her in these words:

> My child, God has endowed you with a noble voice. I have done for you all I can do. You are ready to appear before the world. Go, my child, and my blessing go with you. I shall live to behold in you the first singer in Europe.

Her success was immense, and she came to America crowned with honors; her progress everywhere was a continued ovation. She was supported by Signor Tierieni, the great tenor, and Count Paul Julien. Her engagement lasted a week, her repertoire being "La Semiramide," "Il Frugallo," "La Favorita," "Don Giovana," and "La Nozze de Figaro." She crowded the houses at triple prices.

EDWIN BOOTH.

Mr. Edwin Booth next appeared for the first time at the National as "King Richard the III.," with Mrs. Germon as the Dutchess of York. This lady soon became a great favorite with the Washingtonians, and they in a measure adopted her, and she was always sure of a warm welcome whenever she appeared.

A great deal of interest was manifested by the Washington public to witness Edwin Booth's debut. His father, Junius Brutus, was the central figure—the sun, as it were, of the English stage—around whom revolved many luminaries.

Among the opponents of hereditary genius, it was said that his son could not inherit his father's gift. A mother may transmit to her offspring her mental qualities, but a father never.

These doubters came to the theater prepared to score a knockdown proof of the truth of their theory, and the young Edwin had a trying ordeal in appearing before an audience who remembered the superb acting of Junius Brutus Booth, in "Richard the Third" peculiarly, one of his masterly creations. Before the play was half over young Edwin conquered critics, doubters, and habitues alike. As great as was his illustrious father, the son stood his peer every inch. Not only he, but his ill-starred brother John Wilkes, inherited in a great degree his father's gifts.

Edwin Booth is the pride and ornament of the American stage, he stands in his Auleleun majesty the finest Anglo Saxon artist alive. In person he is ideally handsome and has the glowering luminous eyes, the speaking face, the changeful voice, vast in volume, and of marvellous flexibility and range. As a tragedian he compares to Edmund Kean. He is the only Hamlet in the world; as Claude Melnotte he is entrancing and fascinating beyond what words can tell, he gives to love-language numberless shades, gentle, *naive*, tender, tragic grace.

His Richelieu is nature's self; he never oversteps the bounds; no measured and artificial cadences; no unnatural pauses; no affectation, but the great Cardinal, albeit but a weak old man, rises in his majesty, and shows us at last the secret of his mighty power, which made him the master of France, against all '' steel, poison, malice, domestic and foreign levy.''

NEW NATIONAL THEATER.

KUNKEL & CO. ....LESSEES
JOHN T. FORD..MANAGER
(Also of Holiday St. Theater, Balto., **Richmond**, Va., Theatre, and Portsmouth, Va., **Theatre.**)
STAGE MANAGER..MR. I. B. PHILLIPS
JOHN WELLS..TREASURER

PRICES OF ADMISSION.

Dress Circle and **Parquette**..50 cts.
Procenium Boxes ....$8 and $10 00
Orchestra Chairs..$1 00
Reserved Seats...75 cts.
Private Boxes..$5 00
Family Circle..25 cts.
Colored Boxes..50 cts.
Colored Gallery..25 cts.

THIRD SHAKESPEAREAN EVENING.

Fifth Appearance and Benefit of the eminent Young Tragedian,

MR. EDWIN BOOTH,

Who for the first time presents his name to a Washington Audience as a Beneficiary.

Friday evening, November 21, 1856, will be presented Shakespeare's great Play entitled the

MERCHANT OF VENICE.

SHYLOCK..MR. EDWIN BOOTH
Antonio..Mr. H. A. Langdon
Gratiano..W. H. Briggs
Lorenzo..T. Shirley
Bassanio...W. H. Bokee
Old Gobbo..W. Ellis
Launcelot...Mr. Jos. Parker
Portia..Mrs. Phillips
Nerissa...Miss Josephine Parker
Jessica..Miss Ellen Morant

FANCY DANCE..MISS ELLA WARREN

HISTORY OF THE NEW NATIONAL THEATER. 41

After which the delightful Shakespearean Comedy of
TAMING THE SHREW!

PETRUCHIO	Mr. E. Booth
Grumio	Mr. Jos. Parker
Baptista	Mr. W. H. Bokee
Brondello	Mr. Church
Hortensio	Mr. Van Osten
Music Master	Mr. Hight
Pedro	Mr. Germon
Tailor	Mr. Phillips
Katherine (first time)	Mrs. Phillips
Bianca	Mrs. Hight
Curtis	Mrs. Germon

On to-morrow (Saturday) evening, MR. BOOTH'S FAREWELL! When he will appear as SIR EDWARD MORTIMER, in Colman' Great Play of "THE IRON CHEST!" and in the glorious Comedy of LITTLE TODDLEKINS!

In active preparation the gorgeous Fairy Spectacular Drama, entitled
THE NAIAD QUEEN;
OR, THE NYMPHS OF THE RHINE!

With entirely new and magnificient scenery, by the celebrated Artist, CHAS. S. GETZ, Esq. Elaborate and Intricate Machinery, by Messrs Gardiner & Smith. Splendid Costumes, by Mrs. Whalen, Glenn, Williams and others. During the piece, Grand Marches by sixteen Lovely Girls, arrayed in costly and beautiful Armors, as Female Warriors. Doors open at 6¾, the curtain will rise at 7¼ o'clock.

MISS FANNY MORANT, MANAGERESS.

Still another change of managers. The *Intelligencer* of the date of December 29, 1856, presents the card of Miss Fannie Morant, informing the public that she has become the lessee and directress of the National Theater.

Miss Morant was not only an actress of fine talent, but a thorough business woman withal. She evidently intended to stay, for she changed the title of the house to Fanny Morant's National Theater, and led off as Peg Woffington, in "Masks and Faces."

SECOND DESTRUCTION OF THE THEATER BY FIRE.

January 12, 1856, saw another year dawn upon the theatre, and Mr. John E. Owens and Mrs. Melinda Jones celebrated it by appearing in the comedy of "Self," followed by the farce of "A Kiss in the Dark." As the curtain fell upon the unthinking multitude indulging in uproarious merriment, none could have guessed that it would never rise again. The players, fagged out, hastily donned their daily costume, washed the paint and powder from their faces, and hurried to their hotel, never stopping to cast a glance behind at the building, which they would never see again. The silence of night fell, the lights were out, and on the stage no living footsteps would ever fall It may be the shades of tragedy stalked solemnly along, bidding adieu to the scenes of its many triumphs, and comedy might have passed across the silent boards, for once, its bright face grave, and its laughing eyes heavy with tears.

The old National's day had come; its hour had struck, and the incendiary's torch was lighted.

At three o'clock it was set on fire, and in a few hours nothing but its bare walls remained. No lives were lost, no one was hurt; indeed throughout all the reverses of fortune the National has been the especial pet of the Goddess of Fortune. Fate could destroy it, but its good luck ever remained. During all of its existence for over a half a century, no person was ever killed or injured with-

BOX OFFICE.—LOBBY VIEW.

in its walls. Once inside its doors, every life was a charmed one, neither flood or fire could harm it. There is no theater in America with such a record.

"The fire this time," said Mr. Moxley, "began in the property room, which was upstairs, and I was in the theater when it caught. I shall not forget the excitement. A New York party was about to produce a spectacle called 'Olympic Devils,' and we were getting up the scenery and properties for the piece."

The following card appeared in the *Intelligencer*, February 9, 1856:

> The actors and actresses, sufferers by the fire on Friday evening, appeal in their emergency to the generosity of the public, asking a favorable response to their invitation on Tuesday evening at Odd Fellows' Hall, when an attractive entertainment will be given, and a good opportunity for rendering material aid and comfort to many who were in a moment rendered destitute of their all.

For six years the dismantled walls of the National was all that remained to mark its site. For a couple of years after its destruction there was a financial depression that swept over the country, and retarded all works of improvements, especially upon those buildings that were not indispensable. No profession feels "hard times" so severely as the dramatic, and when people are forced to economize they always commence with dispensing with their amusements.

Another fact miltitated against the erection of the National. The Presidential election was rapidly approaching, and the sectional bitterness that was smouldering between the north and south threatened soon to break out in open flame. In that case, capitalists feared that Washington would be the bone of contention between the two contestants, and it would suffer the fate of a conquered city. In other words the National Capital was too close to the border of the Slave States to be secure and safe, and the property owners were very near a panic, and never was real estate and houses so cheap as during the three years preceding the civil war. In 1859, '60, and '61, building operations were almost at a stand still, every one was uncertain of the Capital's future, and so, among the thousands of eligible building situations in the city that remained unimproved, the National was one of them.

At the threshold of the civil war, people were two much excited to attend a mimic represertation, when the curtain was slowly rolling up on a stage that was a continent, whose actors were a nation, and the scenes and tableaux were sieges and battles, fearfully realistic. The first year of conflict, the Capital was in constant danger of conquest, and the booming of the Southern cannon at Munson's Hill, but a few miles away, sounded a warning menace that prevented any building enterprise in the city.

Another year passed; all was changed, events succeeded each other so rapidly in the war period that impossibilities became facts. A mighty army protected the National Capital, an army whom the people looked upon as invincible; money was so plentiful that it floated everywhere, and now that Washington was safe, and the headquarters of a mighty Nation engaged in war, and filled with the civil and military agents of the Government, all flush of funds, the city jumped upwards in population and wealth like the towns of a rich mining camp. The artizan's trowel and hammer were heard all day long and far into the evening. Real estate made the fortunes of those who early invested in it; and trebled in value in a few months. In these war times the craving for excitement became chronic, the people and the soldiers wanted to be amused, the horrors around them demanded an antidote, and consequently the houses of amusement were packed.

In the mean time the property had passed through various hands, and a portion of the ground now occupied by the theater buildings had been sold to Allison Nailor. The board of managers had changed in several respects, and among those who participated on one side or the other in the various deeds of trust were Thomas J. Semmes, W. D. Davidge, J. B. H. Smith, Wm. H. Winder, A. Hyde, Thomas R. Sutor, James A. and John T. Lenman. A decree of sale was made by the equity court June 13, 1856, and W. D. Davidge and Charles Wallach were made trustees. No sale was made, however, at the time, and on the breaking out of the war Mr. Wallach went south, Mr. John F. Ennis was substituted in his place as trustee, and in 1863, Messrs. Davidge and Ennis sold the entire property to W. E. Spaulding and W. W. Rapley for $35,100.

CHAPTER IV.

THE FOURTH OPENING.—LEONARD GROVER, MANAGER.

So it was that the National was re-built on a larger, more commodious and expensive scale than ever before. It was finished in the spring of 1862.

The following appears in the *Evening Star*, under date of April 23, 1862:

GROVER'S THEATER.

The old National Theater is again destined to shine in all its former glory. Mr. W. E. Spaulding has erected the New National, without regard to cost, upon the site of the old building, and has leased it for a term of years to the popular and energetic manager, Mr. Leonard Grover. This building as completed has a capacity for about two thousand people. The ceiling and walls are elegantly frescoed and the boxes neatly and tastefully painted and panelled. The scenery is from the pencil of Getz. To sum it all up, Mr. Spaulding has erected the largest, most comfortable, and most eligibly located theater in the city.

PROGRAMME GROVER'S THEATER (OLD NATIONAL.)

LEONARD GROVER................................ Sole Lessee and Manager

GRAND OPENING NIGHT AND INAUGURAL PERFORMANCE.
This evening, April 22, 1862.
THE SERIOUS FAMILY.
AND THE FARCE J. J., OF THE WAR DEPARTMENT.

As played by the most brilliant comedy combination that has ever appeared on the American stage. Inaugural overture by the entire Marine band of thirty-two performers, who have generously offered their services for the new theater's initial performance. Miss Lettie Parker, Miss Sophia Gimber, Mrs. J. Germon, Miss Julia Nelson, Mrs. Hand, Mrs. J. S. Edwards, Miss Bramaire, Miss Williams, and a large and beautiful corps de ballet have volunteered their services for the occasion; also Messrs. Daniel Setchel, E. L. Tilton, R. S. Meldrum, H. B. Phillips, J. S. Edwards, J. Seymour, J. M. Ward, William Baker, L. Martin, N G. Hill, and a complete corps of auxiliaries have offered their services. The Marine band will, between the acts, perform grand balcony concerts.

PRICES OF ADMISSION.

Orchestra boxes	$10 00
Orchestra Chairs	1 50
Orchestra Circle	1 00
Dress Circle	75
Gallery	25

The *Star* says of this entertainment:

Mr. Grover opened the house with an elegant and popular combination of artistic dramatique. Miss Hough did well. We need not allude to the genius of Mrs. Germon; her talent in comic parts is too well known to speak of here. She received several encores. The opening night was a grand success.

MAD. ELENA D'ANGRI.

On Monday, May 5, 1862, came L. M. Gottschalk, pianist, in conjunction with Grau's Italian Opera Troupe, with Madame Elena D'Angri, soprano, and Signor Brignoli, the renowned tenor. "La Favorita" was produced, with the result, of course, of a full house.

ANNIE LOUISE KELLOGG.

On May 30, 1862, Miss Annie Louise Kellogg stepped for the first time before the footlights of the National, in the opera of "Lucia di Lammermor."

This opera closed the season, which was the most prosperous one the theater had ever known.

MR. AND MRS. W. J. FLORENCE.

September 15, 1862, Mr. and Mrs. Florence in "Born to Good Luck." This ran a week, and was followed by "Damon and Pythias," with Mr. E. L. Davenport as the star.

LUCILLE WESTERN.

Miss Lucille Western commenced an engagement without a precedent in the history of the National, her "Camille" took the city by storm, and she played to good houses for six consecutive weeks.

YANKEE ROBINSON.

The end of the year 1862 was marked by the first appearance of Yankee Robinson, in a new military comic drama called "The Times of '76; or, The Days That Tried Mens' Souls." This piece, full of patriotic songs and sentiments, was a great favorite with the soldiers, and many a gallant fellow spent a week in the guard house for "running the blockade" to witness it.

The Old National did a rushing business, and the managers and actors in these "piping days of peace," often look back regretfully upon the flush times of the war, when everybody had money in their pockets, and spent it freely. Those days when it took a heavy detachment of local police to keep in order the long line of soldiery and citizens, who jammed the streets, waiting for the theater doors to open.

THE YEAR OF 1863.—ANNIE PROVOST

On January 5, 1863, Miss Annie Provost made her first dramatic debut in Washington, in Charles Reade's comedy of "Nell Gwynne," and concluded with a neat afterpiece written by Manager Grover, called "Cape May Diamonds."

Barney Williams and wife, and Laura Keene's "Comedy Congress," followed each with a week's engagement, and on March 16th, E. L. Davenport and J. W Wallack joined forces and started with a very strong company. Emily Mestayer and Ada Parker being also in the company. They played Shakespearean roles only.

In April the theater had Misses Susan Denin and Annette Ince, playing "Romeo and Juliet," the latter well portrayed, but with Romeo personated by a woman the love scenes rather languished. Romeo's duel with the fiery Tybalt was a remarkable performance. His deadly thrusts consisted of a series of feminine pokes, more suggestive of the housemaid's routing a lazy dog from the hearth rug with the broom handle, than the keen rapier seeking the foeman's heart.

JOHN WILKES BOOTH.

On Saturday April 11, 1863, the announcement is made that the distinguished young actor, John Wilkes Booth, will make his first appearance in Washington as "King Richard the III."

A very large and fashionable audience greeted him, and, a singular coincidence, President Lincoln and Senator Oliver P. Morton occupied a private box. As the great Lincoln sat there, heartily applauding the young actor, how little he imagined that he beheld his fate, and the delicate hand that handed the signet ring in play to the Governor of the Tower, was destined to hold the fatal weapon that was to end his own life at a time when he had climbed the very pinnacle of human greatness.

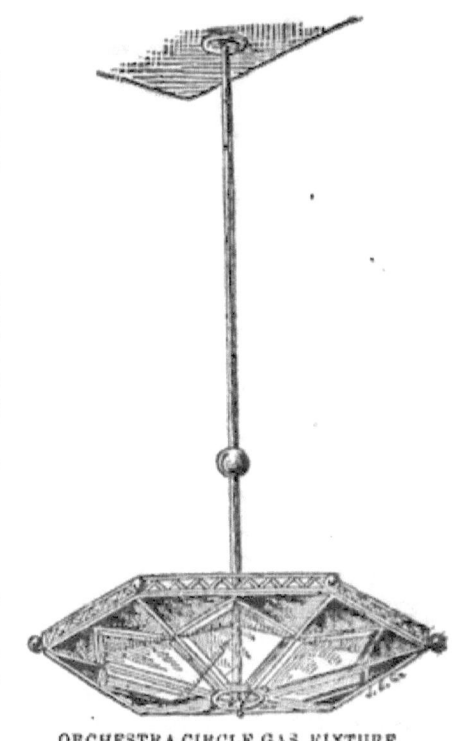

ORCHESTRA CIRCLE GAS FIXTURE.

Mr. J. Wilkes Booth played but one engagement in this house, the occasion referred to. After considerable trouble and research we were enabled to procure the play bill of that engagement, and here reproduce it:

NATIONAL THEATRE.

LEONARD GROVER .... Sole Lessee and Manager.

First appearance of the distinguished young actor,
J. WILKES BOOTH
IN HIS CELEBRATED CHARACTER OF DUKE OF GLOSTER,
AFTERWARDS RICHARD III.
Saturday evening April 11, Shakespeare's Tragedy,
RICHARD III;
OR, THE BATTLE OF BOSWORTH FIELD.

RICHARD III	J. WILKES BOOTH
Richmond	E. H. Brink
King Henry	William Bailey
Buckingham	S. K. Chester
Norfolk	C. Williams
Prince of Wales	Mrs. Edwards
Duke of York	Miss Susie Parker
Stanley	Mr. Stevens
Catesly	J. Edwards
Lord Mayor	J. Parker
Ratcliffe	W. Barron
Oxford	Mr. Acker
Blunt	Mr. Kilbourn
Lieut of Tower	H. Wybroy
Tirrell	Mr. Hillyard
Queen Elizabeth	Miss Alice Grey
Lady Anne	Miss Effie Germon
Duchess of York	Mrs. Muzzy

Several troupes of no great celebrity played at the National, and the season was ended on July 8th by a benefit to the attaches of the theater—Miss Susan Denin, Mr. C. B. Bishop, and Miss Jennie Gourley.

CHAPTER V.

THE FIFTH OPENING.

For nearly a year the proprietors, Messrs. Spaulding and Rapley, had a large force at work on the National, and they spent thousands of dollars in its renovation.

The following card appears in the daily papers:

WASHINGTON, Sept. 24, 1864.

Since the close of the summer season, the proprietors of this building, Messrs. Spaulding and Rapley, have been making alterations and improvements, nearly amounting to the reconstruction of the edifice. Mr. Grover remains lessee of the New National. The work of the proprietors was done under the immediate supervision of those excellent builders Messrs. Entwisle and Barron.

THE YEAR OF 1864.—MAD. PONISI.

The National, newly renovated, decorated, painted and lighted, threw open its spacious doors on the opening night, September 5, 1864, with the William Warren Combination which played for two weeks and was followed by the European tragedienne Madame Ponisi, as the Marquise de Pompadour, in the five act play of "Narcisse." E. L. Davenport played in October with a strong troupe, the drama being the "Iron Mask," and the next month Mr. and Mrs. J. W. Wallack gave the tragedy of the "Gamester."

The first of December found the Ravel Troupe delighting their audiences by their wonderful feats of skill.

Christmas week was a gala one at the National. A spectacular play called "The Relief of Lucknow," in which there was enough burnt powder, blue lights and sulphur to suit even the soldiers who had just come from the front.

THE YEAR OF 1865.—AVONIA JONES.

The opening of the year 1865 was marked by the advent of no less a person than the celebrated Miss Avonia Jones in the part of "Leah the Forsaken." This Miss Jones was the daughter of Count Johannes Jones, the eccentric actor, and this was her last engagement in this city. At her benefit she presented "Romeo and Juliet." J. Wilkes Booth playing Romeo to her Juliet.

Vestvali, or the Magnificent, as she was called, or called herself, gave a week in running one tragical play called "The Jewish Mother."

All of this fog of mediocrity was cleared away by the brilliant sun of Booth, who opened in the latter part of March, finely supported by such fine stock actors and actresses as Messrs. J. J.

Prior, Charles Barron, Miss Alice Placide, and Miss Shelton, "Hamlet" was given magnificently, both in acting and in mounting

Grover's Grand German Opera, in "Faust," came next with twenty-three artists, and a large and thoroughly drilled chorus.

Then followed successively Davenport, in "Othello;" Mary Probst. in the "Hunchback;" Charlotte Thompson, as "Little Barefoot;" George Kunkel, as "Uncle Tom and his Cabin." The latter gave matinees, with the price fixed at 30 cents to any and all parts of the house.

The last play in this season, was Miss Kate Vance, who, with her educated horse Don Juan, appeared in a play called "Mazeppa; or, the Wild Horse of Tartary."

President Lincoln had the offer of a box during this engagement, and on the evening of his assassination he had almost determined to accept it, and given up the idea of going to Ford's. Unhappy decision; had he gone to the National, he would perchance be alive to-day, the most beloved of all Americans.

The following card was issued by the managers on the occasion of the assassination:

> The manager deems it proper to announce that in view of the terrible calamity which has befallen our country in the untimely death of our beloved President, he considers it meet and proper that the National shall remain closed until the general grief which overshadows our community shall have subsided. Therefore we close the theater indefinitely.

WILLIAM H. CRANE.

The Holman Opera Troupe opened the fall season; among them was a young comedian, William H. Crane, who afterwards achieved fame and fortune in conjunction with Stuart Robson.

James E. Murdoch began the period by playing Rover, in "Wild Oats." Mrs. D. P. Bowers, succeeded him with a fair play, called "Loves Sacrifice," in which the heroiness gives up a brown stone front, a cottage by the sea, a pair of bays and an opera box, all for love, and marries the poor young man. We rarely indeed see this loves sacrifice, except on the boards by gaslight.

THE YEAR OF 1866.

Maggie Mitchell, like the theater rejuvenated, repainted, and as bright as a dollar, opened January 8th, with a three weeks engagement, playing "Fanchon," the "Cricket" and "Little Barefoot" alternately.

MR. AND MRS. CHARLES KEAN.

Mr. and Mrs. Barney Williams played for several weeks to overflowing houses, and were followed by Mr. and Mrs. Charles Kean who performed the latter part of March in "Henry the VIII." The play was finely mounted and well acted. The prices during Mr. Kean's performances were doubled.

HISTORY OF THE NEW NATIONAL THEATER. 51

In May the announcement is made that the talented young Washingtonian, J. Newton Gotthold, will make his first appearance in this city as "Othello." His name was a good one, but he never got hold of Washington's public patronage, for he did not appear in this theater again.

In the month of May, Holman's Juvenile-Opera Troupe played Cinderella—chiefly to nurses and children. Cotton and Murphy's minstrel show held out for a week.

JOHN T. FORD, MANAGER.

LOTTA.

On June the first, Mr. John T. Ford took temporary charge of the National, and brought out that champagne-cocktail of the profession, Miss Lotta, who turned the heads and even the hearts of the Washingtonians. She was assisted by Mr. Theodore Hamilton, his first appearance here. He had been a soldier in Lee's army, and no doubt enjoyed the mimic splendor of the stage, and sweet music of the orchestra, better than standing a lonely vigil on picket duty in a blinding rain, or being chased by a score of blue coats through fen and fallow. Mr. Hamilton was for years a most popular actor with the Washingtonians.

In July, Lubin Brothers, necromancers and scientific illusionists, illustrated their proficiency in the dark art. This engagement closed the theater.

SPAULDING & RAPLEY, MANAGERS.

The fall and winter season of 1866, was inaugurated first by a card to the public stating that Grover's National Theater would resume its former name of the "National," with Spaulding and Rapley as proprietors, and J. R. Spackman as stage manager.

In October Mrs. F. W. Lander played Pauline, in the "Lady of Lyons."

The latter part of the month F. S. Chanfrau made his second appearance in Washington, in the original production of "Sam," his success was marvellous, and he struck a new and unique vein, full of true pathos and humor, and the people responded to those touches of nature, and thronged the theater.

The ever popular Opera Troupe, Richings, wound up the last month of October.

Tragedy succeeded the opera, and Mr. J. W. Wallack, as "Hamlet" "still unpacked his heart with words."

JOSEPH JEFFERSON.

November brought Mr. Jefferson to the National—not now as in the past, a combined manager, treasurer, doorkeeper or anything, now ready to play any part to fill up any needed chink. Instead he came a conqueror, he had climbed from the bottom to the eminence of the first comedian of America. His "Bob Acres," and "Caleb Plummer," crowded the theater

RISTORI.

In December the lovers of the drama had a real treat in store for them, the greatest living actress was soon to grace and honor the stage of the National with her presence. Ristori's repetoire was "Medea," "Mary, Queen of Scotts," "Queen Elizabeth," and "Marie Antoinette." Her fine physique, noble carriage, wonderful facial expression, made her great in posing and pantomime. Her versatility was wonderful. In her several death scenes she acted all differently. Her dramatic passion at times was sublime. In the second act of "Medea" (her favorite role), after the scene with Jason, she falls upon a seat frantic with anger and grief; her sobs were so heart rendering, her agony so unutterably pitiable that their was literally not a dry eye in the theater.

ORCHESTRA RAIL AND PILLAR.

Ristori has been compared often to Rachel. They frequently played against each other in Paris. Guizot admirably described the two. Rachel is the *beau ideal* of an aristocratic tragic actress and Ristori the *beau ideal* democratic actress.

The National was squeezed tight with a most enthusiastic audience. Ristori's engagement was a magnificent ovation from first to last, and those who were so fortunate as to see her, knew that she might possibly be equalled, but the world could not produce her superior. Her "Marie Antoinette" was sublime and infinitely touching; her "Mary, Queen of Scots," was perfection itself. One could understand that sovereignty of beauty which swayed men's wills, and the Circean power that made them die for the frail, but surpassingly fascinating queen.

THE YEAR OF 1867.

The new year of 1867 found Mr. Jefferson recalled to Washington, and on New Year's night he gave to the public of this city—for the first time—that immortal creation, "Rip Van Winkle." A greater, more tender, more lovable character never enthralled an audience, or melted them in tears. Of course every seat was filled, and every foot of ground in the aisles occupied.

Certainly the winter of 1866-7 was the most brilliant ever witnessed in Washington. Wallack, Davenport, Lotta, Vestvali, Mrs. Lander, Chanfrau, The Richings' Opera, Jefferson, the great Ristori, and Max Maretzeks' Grand Italian Opera.

In February, Mrs. F W. Lander, appeared as "Adrienne the Actress," for two weeks.

Edwin Forrest appeared for ten nights.

Age had only enhanced his talents; for as years past had brought the philosophic mind, they tempered and refined the animal fierceness, strained out the crudity and excess, and a true imaginative portraiture took the place of sensational realizing. He played the role for the first time here of "Richelieu," with Miss Lillie as Julie D'Mortimer.

JOHN BROUGHAM.

March 4, 1867, Mr. John Brougham, the poet-author and playright—as well as comedian—makes his first appearance as Dr. Savage, in his own original comedy, in four acts, entitled, "Playing with Fire."

After him came John E. Owens, with an engagement of six nights, the play being "Dot; or, The Cricket on the Hearth."

Miss Rachael Johnson then appeared as Lady Isabel, in "East Lynne." She was supported by Mr. B. Macauley.

JULIA DALY.

In April, Miss Julia Daly, who had won a national reputation as a comic actress, made a hit in the play of "Our Female American Cousin." She drew fair sized audiences throughout the week.

Mr. Wallack followed in an entirely new play entitled, "A Dangerous Game."

Miss Lucille Western scored a splendid success as Lady Isabel, in "East Lynne." All other stars "paled their ineffectual fires" before her. She was the original wedded maid and widowed wife of the great novel and play—the others only copies.

J. S. CLARKE.

J. S. Clarke, the capital comedian, scored an undiminished success in "Toodles," and as Major Wellington De Boots, in "Everybody's Friend."

The Richings' Grand Opera followed with a very strong troupe. Wm. Castle, the sweetest American tenor that ever sang; S. C. Campbell, the baritone so rich and full, whose Beppo in "Fra Diavolo" can never be forgotten; H. C. Peakes, and little Mrs. Zelda Seguin, with her pretty face and exquisite contralto.

They played a week to full houses, and by a general request they extended their time six nights more—a compliment that the Washington public—the most critical on earth—rarely give to any one.

The fall opening, September 16, 1867, was commenced by the Richings' Opera Troupe, with a three weeks' engagement. They met with deserved success.

October 8th found Chanfrau as "Sam," playing a two weeks' engagement. He also gave his unequalled imitations of Booth, Keene, Williams, and his "take-off" of Bob Brierly, in the "Ticket-of-Leave-Man," brought down the house.

Ristori, the sublime, in "Elizabeth" and "Marie Antoinette," and none but a woman of transcendent genius could faithfully portray her queens—the very antipodes of each other.

Maggie Mitchell followed in "Fanchon," and after her came the burly-rolling tub-of-intestines, honest Jack Falstaff, with the "only" Hackett in the title role.

Edwin Forrest played a two weeks engagement in his famous and familiar roles. He brought out "Matamoras," this appearance.

Full houses greeted John Brougham during his two weeks stay at the National. David Copperfield dramatized, with Brougham as the immortal Micawber. Also "A Gentleman from Ireland."

THE YEAR OF 1868.—THE AGE OF OPERA BOUFFE.

Tragedy, comedy, farce, and the opera had alternately amused, interested or excited the people, and now there was a new departure, and a new era in music. The majestic statue of art was to be adorned with the Jester's cap and bells, and the Bacchante was to be crowned with the laurel of Melpomone, and the oak of Thalia.

HISTORY OF THE NEW NATIONAL THEATER. 55

W. L. Bateman, with his Parisian Opera Bouffe, opened January, 1868, at the National, with Offenbach's, "Grand Duchess." The novelty drew crowds, and the capricious fancy of the public was completely captivated, and "Opera Bouffe" was now the furore and rage for a long time.

February, Mikado's Japanese Troupe gave entertainments well worth seeing.

The three months of March, April and May, 1868, passed with three celebrities at the National. Maggie Mitchell, in "Little Barefoot;" Joe Jefferson, as "Rip Van Winkle," and three farewell performances of Madame Adelaide Ristori, before her departure for Europe. When the curtain fell on her last night performance, it did not rise again until the regular autumn season.

When the curtain, gliding up on the night of September 7th, it showed the glittering spectacle and enchantments of the "Black Crook," its first appearance in Washington, and the public curiosity was so great, that nearly every desirable seat was bought up at the box office before night.

Offenbach's Comic Opera then held undisputed sway for some weeks.

Christmas week was one of delight to those who loved pure opera. Max Maretzek, with Madame La Grange and corps of artists gave the Italian and German Opera with fine effect, and the old year died with its lasts moments soothed by the exquisite tones of La Grange and Signor Brignoli, that mingling in dulcet harmony formed a fitting requiem to old '68.

THE YEAR OF 1869.

The year 1869, was inaugurated by the advent of the Chapman Sisters, in the musical burlesque of "Cinderella." Another brace of talented sisters, appears and drew only moderately well, they were styled the Zavistowski Sisters, and rendered "Ixion, or the Man at the Wheel," and the romantic drama of "The Dumb Girl of Genoa."

Joe Jefferson then appears, with "Rip Van Winkle," which he used to say he was sick and tired to death of, that the monotony was maddening, but as the public never wearied of it, he kept on in a ding dong here-we go-style, purely as a matter of business, and piled up the ducats.

In April the Hanlon Brothers in their astonishing gymnastic feats.

In the beginning of May, Dan Bryant's Ministrel Troupe made a decided hit. They gave operas entire, with Dan as the soprano. A morning paper says the performance was "Il Trovatore," which would have astonished Verdi if he had heard it.

The lovers of the Shakespearean drama, who turn up their noses at the opera bouffe, sniff at the minstrels, and religiously keep away from the spectacular which did the bare legged ballet, now hasten to the theater to see Mrs. Scott Siddons make her debut as Rosalind, in "As You Like It." The critics say Mrs. Siddons was handsome, graceful and pleasing as Rosalind, but her acting was occasionally marred by mannerisms.

On May 27th the theater was closed for the summer by a benefit to the attaches of the National. Messrs. Joseph Sessford, Parker, Buckingham, Vesey and Jamison. They were made happy by a first-class house.

The National was opened on September 11th by Leffingwell's Burlesque Combination, the play being the "Gushing Clorinda."

The ever warmly welcomed Richings' Opera Troupe came next with the usual result.

This seemed a flush year for minstrel shows, for another turns up called Newcomb's Burlesque Artists, with Joe Emmet, the Dutch delineator, as an attraction. The papers spoke highly of their performance.

In November, Mlle. Rita Sangalli and her troupe was billed to play the fairy burlesque called "Flick-Flock." The papers the next morning remark:

It was a disastrous and complete failure and mortifying break-down, owing to the non-arrival of the music from Baltimore in time for rehearsal.

ROSE AND HARRY WATKINS.

In November, Rose and Harry Watkins played a dramatization of Ouidas famous novel, "Under Two Flags," and Rose Watkins' rendition of the sparkling, bewitching, little devil, Cigarette, was perfection herself. The house was crowded.

Maurice Grau now comes with his Grand German Opera, with a whole host of artists with jaw cracking names. The critic of the *Chronicle* said the next morning:

"The Magic Flute performance last night did not strike us very favorably in consequence of the lack of ensemble."

If you have tears prepare to shed them now, for here comes Lucille Western to unlock the founts, or, as Sam Weller would say, turn the water-works on. Her conception of Lady Isabel was good, but her Madame Vine in "East Lynne," was the saddest, most sorrowful rendition of human grief and despair that was seen on the boards of the National for a long time. "East Lynne" ran for two weeks.

The closing year of 1869, found Mr. and Mrs. Claude Hamilton in the melodrama, "The Murder by the Roadside Inn."

THE YEAR OF 1870.

Mr. and Mrs. Florence opened the year of 1870 by the "Colleen Bawn."

MISS BATEMAN

Engagement for six nights of the celebrated American tragedienne, Miss Bateman, is what meets our eye on the bill boards on the streets. She played the character of Mary Warner, in the play of that title, supported by Mr. George Jordan. President Grant and wife, Generals Porter and Sherman, were present. The announcement that General Sherman was present is superfluous, for as regularly as the week came around he proceeded to the National, his long ungainly form, whimsical face, and shrewd eyes was familiar to the *habitues* of the pit. He was always democratic to the core, hated boxes, despised form, and went to enjoy the play as one of the people, not as a big general with a noisy staff. General Grant was so frequent a visitor to the theater, that his presence never excited remark, and rarely produced a local notice in the papers.

Another Burlesque Opera Company, Lingard's, in the "Captain of the Watch." They were well received.

A rush to the box office, and a double price for a seat marks the advent of Max Maretzek's Grand Italian Opera Company. Brial, Lumley, Lefranc, &c.

DRESS CIRCLE STAIRWAY.

The criticism by the press on "Trovatore," is that Signor Lefranc has a voice of rare purity and power, but that the Prima Donna Madame Brial's voice lacks freshness, and appears worn and strained. No mention is made of the lesser lights.

The "Horse Opera," for the twentieth time. Burnt cork seems to be king, and any man in the Union who can sing a song or pick the banjo, straightway joins a minstrel show The years 1869 and '70, were prolific of these combinations the public taste set that way, and "*Il faut que le publique S'amuse.*" Kelly & Leons' combination of burnt corkers, gave a burlesque entitled, "Matrimony."

February 7th, E. L Davenport, for a week, roles "Hamlet" and "A New Way to Pay Old Debts." Maggie Mitchell, in the "Pearl of Savoy," for two weeks to only moderate houses.

The spring of 1870 was marked by the return of many of the old favorites. Mrs. D. P Bowers, in "Lady Audley's Secret;" John Owens, as "Solon Shingle;" Jefferson, as "Rip;" Lotta, in the "Little Detective;" John Brougham, in the "Red Light;" Mrs. Bowers, in "Marie Stuart," and E. L. Davenport, in "The Soldier of Fortune," followed each other consecutively, to good, bad and indifferent houses as the case may be.

The close of the spring season was marked by two benefits. The first was a grand complimentary testimonial to manager Spaulding, on which occasion, Mr. E. L. Davenport, Miss Annette Ince, and Frank Mordant volunteered their services. The comedy was "Faint Heart Never Won Fair Lady."

The night after was another benefit, this time to that popular artiste, Mrs. G. C. Germon, on which occasion the lovely actress, Miss Effie Germon appeared in the role of Jessie Brown, or the "Relief of Lucknow." A big crowd assembled, and Mrs. Germon's friends gave her a fine send off.

JOE K. EMMETT.

On September 26, 1870, Joe Emmet appeared for the first time before the footlights of the National in the role that he had made so famous, as Fritz, in our "German Cousin."

W. E. SPAULDING, MANAGER.

Mr. William E Spaulding announces that he is the sole manager of the National.

Mr. and Mrs. Florence in "Handy Andy."

And then Oliver Doud Byron was heralded as bringing a show worth paying a dollar to witness. It was a real lurid drama called "Across the Continent," and the blue and red lights were in constant demand. People outside the theater thought a battle was going on inside, judging from the rattle of the musketry and shouts of the combatants.

Lucille Western in the "weeping business" again, old role, succeeded by the Ravel Family; and next pretty Miss Lotta, and Mrs. and Mr. Barney Williams, played through November, and the following two weeks were Mrs. Lander and Rose Watkins, the former in "Queen Elizabeth," the latter in "Under Two Flags."

HISTORY OF THE NEW NATIONAL THEATER.

CHARLES FECHTER.

The world renowned actor, Charles Fechter, made his first appearance at the National December 16, 1871, as Claude Melnotte, with Caroline Leclerque as Pauline. He scored a splendid success.

There was no performance for two weeks afterwards in consequence of the extensive arrangements for bringing out the new Christmas pantomime of "See-Saw; or, The old Woman that lived in the Shoe," which had been in preparation for several months past. New scenery, new costumes, new calcium lights, a large chorus, not only showed the tact and enterprise of Mr. Spaulding, the owner, but of Mr. Parker, stage manager, as well.

"The Old Woman that Lived in the Shoe" had a run of several nights and a matinee. Nearly every child in Washington saw this scene from wonderland, and it set every infantile tongue gabbling like mad, and how many hours of sleep the "innocents" lost in consequence, only the tired nurses could tell. It played its final performance on New Year's night.

THE YEAR OF 1871.—MRS. SCOTT SIDDONS.

The following well know stars, gleamed at the National, and then disappeared for a time: Fechter, as "Hamlet," drew crowded houses, and his delineation of the Dane, drew unmeasured praise from press and people. Mrs. Scott Siddons acted as "Romeo," who, by the way, is responsible for many a woman donning that portion of the masculine attire known as pants and breeches.

LYDIA THOMPSON.

Mrs. Bowers, in "Lady Audley's Secret," and Lydia Thompson with her troupe of bare limbed blondes literally set the town on fire, great throngs packed the National. "Lurline" a burlesque, was received, as the bills would say with rapturous applause. The fair kicker Lydia made her engagement a huge success.

MARIE SEEBACH.

Madame Marie Seebach announces herself as the greatest living tragedienne, and played "Mary Stuart" and "Addrienne Lecourreur" for a week, but the memory of Ristori and Matilda Heron in those roles was so fresh and vivid in people's minds that the Madame suffered by the contrast.

Leonora Cavender, played a week to poor houses, in a play called the "Ups and Downs of City Life." People did not require to pay a dollar to see ups and downs, they had them free of charge.

Another sensational play is put upon the boards, called "Neck and Neck," by E. T. Stetson, a youth hitherto unknown to fame. This drama had a very realistic gallows and railroad scene, and people fond of thrills could shiver down to their boot heels at the narrow escapes.

Chanfrau appears with a new play called "Kit;" it attracted overwhelming crowds, and the "Arkansas Traveller" rose to deserved eminence at last.

April 10th, Joe Jefferson still playing "Old Rip" to new people and old friends.

FRANK MAYO.

Succeeding him was Frank Mayo, in the "Streets of New York," and on April 24, 1871, the season was closed by one weeks engagement of Carncross and Dixie's Minstrels. They were an Ethiopian success.

J. G. SAVILLE, MANAGER.

On Friday, August 16th, the theater threw open its doors for the benefit of the Washington Monument Fund, under the auspices of the Washington Literary Association, "The Ticket-of-Leave-Man" was played. As it was in the middle of the dog days, with the thermometer at 89° in the night time, the result was that the theater had held larger audiences in its days.

Florence played one week at the opening in September 23, 1872, and was greeted by a large and enthusiastic audience.

October 1st, Miss Susan Denin and Signorini Antonnini, in the "Palace of Truth." A morning paper speaking in a Pickwickian sense says:

Frank and blunt people who wish to see what results from telling the truth all the time should go and pay attention. Politicians are in no need of the lesson.

Mrs. Bowers, in her role of "Amy Robsart," followed by the Holman Opera Troupe, in the "Grand Duchess," which the press says was well performed, though the Prima Donna, Sallie Holman, was not equal to her part.

October 28, Mr. J. G. Saville, as Elliott Gray, in Lester Wallack's play of "Rosedale." Both the actor and the play met with only indifferent success.

Kate Putnam then came in the "Old Curiosity Shop," and made a very favorable impression.

MAY SAVILLE.

Following them was Joe Proctor and May Saville, in "The Red Pocket Book," a sensational play in the truest meaning of the word.

November 25th, the Fifth Avenue Combination, Mr. Geo. C. Boniface and Miss Georgia Langley, in "Divorce." It did not meet with the success it deserved. It may possibly have recalled unpleasant memories to some people.

LESTER WALLACK.

Lester Wallack came with "Central Park," not the reservation, but a play, and starred it for a week, and then left denouncing the want of taste of the Washington public.

HISTORY OF THE NEW NATOINAL THEATER. 61

"After Dark," by a stock company, then a play called "Fee Fo Fe Fum," by Prof. Davis's Educated Dogs, which attracted more custom than many dramas performed by bipeds.

DION BOUCICAULT.

Dion Boucicault and Miss Agnes Robertson, in that humorous and pathetic comedy, "Arrah Na Pogue." They were greeted by magnificent houses.

The fall season brought many well-known stock actors, but no stars of the first magnitude. Lester Wallack, in "Rosedale;" Charles Matthews, in "Married for Money;" Mrs. Chanfrau, in "Christie Johnson;" Manager Saville, in "Saratoga," and he proved himself a very fair comedian, full of vim, and an actor of great magnetism.

THE YEAR OF 1872.

January, 1872, brought the Grand German Opera with the tenor Wachtel as the attraction. The house was well filled with a critical and cultivated audience, and the universal verdict was one of utter disappointment, and the manager left Washington a wiser and a madder man. He found that he could not impose on the natives by employing a fair tenor and a collection of broken down singers with unpronounciable names, who tried to palm off discord as scientific German music.

Maggie Mitchell, Emmet and Lingard, in their usual roles, came in their turn.

CHRISTINE NILLSON.

The advent of the season was the arrival of Maurice Strackosh's Grand Italian Opera, with the renowned Mad. Christine Nillson, and Signor Brignoli, tenor. Double prices, and a brilliant and appreciative audience. A press notice says:

Madame Christine Nillson as Lucia fully sustained her high reputation and awoke genuine enthusiasm. She was lost in her part, and seemed oblivious of the presence of her audience, with one excusable exception. When the charms of her music seemed to soothe the savage breasts of the attaches of the Japanese Embassy sitters, in the front row, her singing put them all in a profound slumber. This seemed to be too ridiculous to escape the attention of the conscientious artist, and she had great difficulty to keep from giving away to uncontrollable mirth, and proceed with her part.

Monsieur Capoul won golden opinions from the audience, and received several encores.

Next came the Oates' Opera Company, which was good; and then Lydia Thompson with her blondes, which was better, and the seats were all sold.

EMMA SOLDENE.

After them came Emma Soldene's Opera Bouffe Company, which was the best of all, and not even standing room was to be had.

Mrs. John Wood made a hit with her London Comedy Company, in refined burlesque.

The theater was closed June 26, 1872, by Skiff and Gaylord's minstrels.

JANAUSCHEK.

The year of 1872 and '73, was opened by Janauschek, in "Mary Stuart." This actress was in her prime, and neither age or bodily infirmity had come to diminish her great powers. She had intense passion and massive force of mind. Janauschek was given to artistic exaggeration, but her stateliness and pomp carried her through when lesser woman would be swamped. A brilliant and critical audience greeted her, and she achieved a genuine triumph. Her engagement lasted a week.

M'LLE AIMEE.

Now comes the Queen of the Opera Bouffe, M'lle Aimee, in her prime, full of deviltry and grace. The piece was "Barbe Bleue," and as many got in the theater as could wedge themselves in some spot to stand on. The Opera Bouffe is a French invention, and nobody but a French woman with her native abandon, dash, vitality tinged with just enough wickedness to make it piquant, can do it justice. Aimee was made for the Opera Bouffe, and Opera Bouffe was made for her, and so it was a harmonized ensemble.

THE YEAR OF 1873.

THIRD DESTRUCTION OF THE THEATRE BY FIRE.

Alice Oates now appears with her Comic Opera Bouffe Company, and though the much married Alice does finely for an American girl, yet her acting suffers in comparison with Aimee's. As the fair Alice's heels vanished, and the curtain rang down, it was destined never to rise again, for the old National now fell a prey to the fire fiend It was burned the next morning January 28, 1873, at 11 in the morning, and partially destroyed. Nobody was hurt. The upper part of the building was owned by Messrs. Miller and Jones as a billiard saloon, whose tables and effects were damaged to the extent of $3,000. Mr. William W Rapley was the owner of the National Theater; he arrived in town from his residence in Montgomery County, Maryland, but a few moments before the fire. The property cost him $138,000, and the total insurance consolidated was only $40,000, leaving Mr. Rapley $98,000 loser by the conflagation, the origin of which was never ascertained.

The theater was a fine one in every respect, and had a seating capacity of about two thousand. The lessee, Mr. J. G. Saville, had successfully managed it for the past two years, and lost most of his effects in its destruction, as did the Oates' Company, whose wardrobe helped in a humble way to feed the flames.

HISTORY OF THE NEW NATIONAL THEATER.

W. W. RAPLEY, OWNER OF THE NATIONAL.

Many men of medium nerve would have been daunted by such a calamity occurring twice, and losing thousands of dollars each time by the untoward event; but Mr. Rapley's acts proved that he was a man of no ordinary mould. Difficulties and misfortunes only seemed to bring out his determined indomitable will, that burned the brighter when the hour was the darkest. Like Marshall Ney, his genius never shone in its brilliancy until the enemies' guns sounded in his ears, and once on the battle-field he was in his true element. Mr. Rapley lost not a moment in weak repining against fate, or railing at fortune—he might have grit his teeth a little harder—but before the ruins actually had cooled he was rebuilding the theater, and if ever a house literally arose from its ashes, the National was that one. It was burned January 28, 1873, and by September the mason's work was done. In November the carpenters and decorators gathered their tools up and left. The painters and upholsterers took their places, and in the incredible space of a little over four months the spacious building threw open its doors to the public on December 1, 1873. It reads like the doings of the *genii*, conjured up by Aladdin rubbing his wonderful lamp.

Mr. Rapley showed in his invincible determination not to yield to adverse fate, that characteristic, essentially American quality, called pluck, a quality which can surmount all difficulties and accomplish well nigh the impossible.

W. W. Rapley, the owner of the National Theater, and the man to whose indomitable pluck the rapid erection of the present splendid edifice is wholly due, was born in Baltimore, Md., on the 22d of February, 1828. After receiving a common school education, he learned the trade of a blacksmith and coach-trimmer, and became an expert workman; so much so that he came to Washington and aided in the completion of the dome of the capitol, and assisted to place it in position. He remained in this city and first started in business for himself in the old first ward, having a shop on Pennsylvania Avenue near Eighteenth street. His close attention to business and promptness in the performance of his work, soon brought him plenty of custom, while his absence of bad habits and strict economy enabled him to lay by a handsome sum. He then purchased the steamer Guy, one of the ferry-boats running between here and Alexandria, and commanded her himself. As a steamboat captain he became very popular, and as he carried to his new occupation the same characteristics which had brought him success before, he was soon enabled to purchase another boat, and at one time was the owner of three steamers plying upon the Potomac.

His purchase of the National Theater property was the result of accident. He had some surplus money lying idle which he had intended to invest in real estate, but at the commencement of the war there was a perfect panic in that kind of investment here and every one was afraid to risk money, not knowing what might be the fate of the capital city. When the theater property was to be sold, Mr. Rapley saw that there was money in the venture, so in connection with Mr. W E. Spaulding, he made the purchase in 1862, and has been identified with the career of the National since that date.

After the fire in 1873, the interest of Mr. Spaulding was purchased by Mr. Rapley, who has from that period been the sole owner of the property.

Mr. Rapley has amassed quite a fortune, which has been judiciously invested. His residence is in Montgomery county, Md., where he has a farm comprising 400 acres of as good land as there is in the State. The house is as elaborately furnished and appointed as any city residence, and here he dispenses the most generous hospitality. Some years ago he started in the stove business, in which enterprise he has been quite successful.

In person, Mr. Rapley is rather below the medium height, but with a compactly built figure, and a countenance every lineament of which shows the energy and determination of his character. Modest and retiring in disposition, he is one of the most genial of men to his friends, while his business sagacity, cool and correct judgment, and his honorable andupright dealings have won for him an enviable position in the community

CHAPTER VI.

THE SIXTH OPENING OF THE NEW NATIONAL.

Extracts from a morning paper:

WASHINGTON, Dec. 1, 1873.

The announcement that the New National Theater has been completely rebuilt, and that the inaugural entertainment will be given this evening, will be hailed with pleasure by the Washington theater-goers.

About the beginning of the war Messrs. Rapley and Spaulding erected a new building on the site of the Old National, but on the 28th of January last, this was destroyed, and Mr. Rapley began the erection of another theater, which should be superior in every respect to any of its predecessors, and is pronounced by all to be one of the finest places of amusement in the country.

The opening night was a gala occasion, and was a brilliant send off. President Grant and Governor Shepherd occupied a box together, and many of the public men of note were present. The queenly Mrs. Sprague, *nee* Miss Kate Chase, occupied a box opposite the President, and looked regal in her blue violet and diamonds. Everything passed off well, and many were the toasts drank that night to the success of Washington's favorite theater.

THE YEAR OF 1874.

The prima donna, Kellogg, started the winter season joyously along, and this young Yankee but a few years before, poor and friendless, with no capital except her own determined will, a flexible sweet voice, and staunch heart, started to climb that hill which, like the mountain in the Arabian Nights, on whose top the key to the magician's treasure hung, and he who would look back was changed into a stone, so the young New Englander climbed when thousands failed, and her success was due more to her singleness of purpose than anything else.

Her engagement commenced January 6th, lasting one week; was a gratifying success, every desirable seat being sold before the doors opened. Lucia was her role, and she gave perfect satisfaction.

Frank Mayo came before a Washington audience for his initial performance in his famous play of "Davy Crockett." The plot of an accomplished and fashionable woman falling madly in love with an ignorant, but handsome and gallant backwoodsman is not improbable, for love knows no law, and since Parthenia tamed Ingomar, the story is always the same. Mayo's conception of the character was excellent, and his delineation very fine indeed. His engagement proved a prosperous one.

Dion Bourcicault followed with a play called, "Used Up," but his Sir Charles Coldstream was not equal to his Irish characters, and he played before very slim houses.

Washington is the heart of the Nation; everybody from everywhere journeys here, sooner or later; all roads "leads to Rome," so all routes center here, and thus, when a play that is damned anywhere else, the intelligence reaches this city and people save their money when they hear a drama or comedy is not up to the mark.

SOTHERN.

The inimitable Sothern, as "Lord Dundreary," made his debut for the first time at the National, and crowds flocked to see him. He became the fashion, and drinks, advertising cards, witicisms, a "la Sothern," was heard on every side.

Mrs. Bowers, next in "Lady Audley's Secret." Mr. Edwin Adams, in "Enoch Arden," successively played to light houses.

Fox and Denier's pantomime had better business, and their "Humpty Dumpty," was an enjoyable piece of farcical extravaganza as was ever witnessed on the boards of the theater.

SALVINI.

The monarch of tempestuous passion now stepped before the footlights for the first time, and Tomaso Salvini gave to delighted and breathless audiences the truest rendition of "Ingomar" they had ever seen.

Salvini was the incarnation of intense dramatic power. His acting was a rare and beautiful combination of contrasting elements conceived by his bright intellect. He aimed at faultless perfection in the minutest details as well as in the lofty grandeurs and comprehensiveness of the general design; he trusted to obtain this by hard work. He once wrote to a young friend of his who had just entered the dramatic profession·

Above all study, study, study, all the genius in the world will not help you along with any art, unless you become a hard student. "It has taken me years to master a single part."

He had a noble bearing and voice of rare beauty, and elocution such as one only hears once in a life time. Beneath his brow full and overreaching, lay great tragic force. Actions are generally more eloquent than words, yet his tones were in sweetness and resonance indescribable. In the three great elements of musical expression, tone, timbre and rhythm, Salvini is the greatest.

He charmed and enthralled his audiences, and scored, as he always did an intellectual conquest.

This grand tragedian in the great play of "Ingomar," was followed by "Uncle Tom's Cabin." A ninety cent fiddle scratching John Brown after a grand cathedral organ performing one of Mozart's creations. "Uncle Tom's Cabin," that play with its mawkish sentimentality and pathos, which the housemaids cry over, and the Africans applaud, was never allowed on the boards of the National but once again.

The theater was closed for the summer by Miss Kate Mayhew, in "With the Tide." The season had been a prosperous one considering the great financial panic.

The fall season of 1874 was opened by Janauschek as "Mary Stuart." Then came Lucille Western in "East Lynne." followed by Ella Wesner in a society play called "Mixed."

Aimee filled the theater, as she always had the knack of doing some decade of years ago. The opera was "La fille de Madame Angot," and it was dashingly played.

ADELAIDE NEILSON.

And now comes the fairest of all fair women who had ever trod the boards of the National—Adelaide Neilson. She came surrounded by her own rosy cloud of love, and the maddening witchery that possessed her, taking the senses by storm, and making men's hearts throb and their pulses beat with ecstacy. Her Juliet was the loveliest ever beheld on earth, and in the balcony scene, when the moonlight gleams on her perfect face, and kisses her Lorelei hair she made a vision that enraptured the eye. Rising from the gutter, yet she was the beau ideal of a proud, patrician. She seemed to show her lineage in her every look, her every tone, her every gesture. She could exclaim with Cleopatra:

And here's my bluest veins to kiss, a hand that kings have lipped, and trembled kissing.

Her Viola was the daintiest creature imaginable. As Perdita she appeared as sweet as Tennyson's Lillian

"So innocent, arch, cunning, simple,
With the baby roses in her cheek."

Her acting was full of tenderness and passion, though it lacked force; but her grace, beauty, and softness on the stage, will never be forgotten.

"The fairness of her face no tongue can tell;
Fairer than the daughters of all human race."

Her end is well-known; taken suddenly ill near Paris a few years ago when riding out, she died in agony on the sofa at a low roadside inn.

In November, J. K. Emmet, as "Fritz," and a full house in consequence.

The Lingard Comedy Company to thin houses; Rose and Harry Watkins in "Trodden Down," and the manager did not count up his receipts that night with much pleasure or profit.

Christmas week, Janauschek for the first time in the new play of "Chesney Wold," a dramatization of Dickens' Bleak House. Her rendition of Lady Dedlock and the Frenchwoman was as fine a piece of acting as could be seen on the English stage.

THE YEAR OF 1875.

On January 20th, the Emma Soldene English Opera Troupe played a week's engagement and made a famous hit. The house was crowded with as many as could possibly get in, and "Madame L'Archi duc" was given with a dash and abandon that caused a round of encores. Emma Soldene was a decided winning card, and she had selected her troupe with rare judgment.

Baker and Farron drew only moderate houses, and February 15, 1875, Katie Putman as "Little Nell," and the "Marchioness," played to a small, but appreciative audience.

On February 22, Strakosh Italian Opera, in "Lohengrin." This opera, while it pleased people of high musical culture, did not take with the masses, and hence it did not pay in this city, at least.

Frank Mayo followed in his old role of "Davy Crockett;" succeeding came Florence, Duprez and Benedict's Minstrels in their olios. Each drawing but indifferently well. Kellogg appeared April 19, to a full house, and gave "Ernani," with fine effect.

Great people generally keep close together, and Ristori follows Kellogg. The queen of tragedy gave a wonderful personation of the "Virgin Queen," she with a woman's heart and man's mind.

On May 3d, the Swiss Bell Ringers gave a week's entertainment to good audiences.

June 21, the theater closed with a benefit to Harold Forsberg.

JOHN T. FORD, MANAGER.

On September 1, 1875, John T. Ford took supreme control of the National.

JOHN M'CULLOUGH.

John McCullough, here makes his debut in the National, as "Hamlet." He was rather too robust and fiery for the portraiture of the philosophical Dane, but still his great genius illumined the part, and made it a creditable one.

John McCullough made many friends in Washington, and he afterwards used to say that he would rather play in this city than any place in the Union.

GEORGE RIGNOLD.

After the genial Mac, as his friends called him, came George Rignold, and like Hotspur, he played havoc with female hearts. In "Henry the Fifth," which was magnificently mounted, he looked "every inch a king," and a more superb specimen of gallant manhood in its prime, was never seen before the footlights. His "Once more to the breach, dear friends; once more for St. George and England," at the siege of Harfleur, was the knightliest picture that was ever witnessed on the American stage. The theater was jammed, and Rignold was the idol of the hour, and the fancy of the fickle populace.

The Vokes family next in their entertaining extravaganza of "The Belles of the Kitchen."

HISTORY OF THE NEW NATIONAL THEATER. 69

Then Mrs. D. P. Bowers in "Lady Audley's Secret," and the week after Mr. Barry Sullivan as "Richelieu," followed by G. H. McDermott, in a new and nonsensical comedy of "Brought to Book."

JOHN T. RAYMOND.

The Christmas holidays were marked by the advent, for the first time, of Raymond's new character, which he has rendered immortal as "Col. Mulberry Sellers." This piece took the town by storm, and the manager waxed more rotund than ever with satisfaction. For a week Raymond kept the town in a roar of laughter, and his dried, shrewd face so often seen in the hotel lobbies, was Sir Mulberry Sellers itself. He had played the part so often that the mannerisms stick to him. He was socially a man of much *bonhomie*, and whenever he strolled out in the day, a crowd of boon companions always surrounded him. Raymond fairly earned his title of the first comedian of America.

THE YEAR OF 1876.

Another sensation that made a hit, and jammed the house, Georgia Langley and Dolly Pike, as the "Two Orphans."

This play was one of the most powerful ones ever written, full of incident and abounding in pathos. It won the popular heart at once, and the theater watched the denouement of the plot with breathless interest, and when the curtain would fall it would be on an audience hushed into silence by the life scenes they had seen portrayed.

CLARA MORRIS.

And now, hats off, for there steps out before the footlights a slight girlish form that is the greatest emotional actress that the New World ever gave to art. A slight swaying figure, a face so wonderfully full of nobility, that the emotions could be read there. A magnetism that conquered everything. A passion so intense and contageous as to thrill a vast body of people like electric shocks. On the 7th of February, 1876, the audience were moved and touched as they never were before when they saw Clara Morris as "Camille."

Her acting was a revelation of the highest point that art can reach. Her dramatic force and power was seen in the quivering play of her hands, the piteous trembling of her lip, the anguished face, the eyes so unutterably sad, and the voice full of unshed tears. Her scornful taunts to her brother, every word of which was a heart string broken. When in the first act of Camille, where she would rush forward and cry aloud, with a bursting heart, "Respect me—and in this house," she made the breast of every man throb with the truest sympathy, and when she parts from her lover, whom she never meant to see again in this world, her anguish and self torture was so heartending that none could look upon Clara Morris save through blinding tears. Her unutterable despair was painful to witness; one forgot the theater, the actress, everything, as the struggle goes on over a laboring soul, and when she dies, people gasps over the death bed scene in sadden horror, as if they had witnessed the demise of one they knew and loved, A press criticism the next morning says:

> Clara Morris shows in "Camille" how thoroughly she identifies herself for the time with the character she takes. The suffused eyes, streaming cheeks, and momentarily changing color of the face, shows that she feels with all the intensity of reality the emotions she depicts.

Little Miss Lotta, in a new play called "Zip," and the archness, freshness and fun of this charming actress, carried all before her, and she never acted with more spirit than she did beneath the roof of the National, a theater she had helped so much to build.

March 20th, Florence in the "Mighty Dollar," and a great success the play proved. Sothern, as Lord Dundreary, and a laughing, joyous audience.

BARRETT, BANGS, DAVENPORT, LEVICK.

Then followed one of the strongest combinations and star cast, and finely mounted plays, any theater ever witnessed. The play "Julius Cæsar," with Milnes Levick in the title role. Lawrence Barrett, as Cassius; E. L. Davenport, Brutus; Frank C. Bangs, as Mark Anthony. This was a fine gathering of stars, and the rendition of the play was well worthy of the galaxy of talent. The house rang with applause, and though the prices were doubled, the theater was filled from gallery to pit. It was a masterly rendition by masterly actors.

MARY ANDERSON.

And now comes the Southern girl from the blue grass region of Kentucky, Mary Anderson, for the first time in the National, in the play of "Evadne." Her freshness, beauty, and high histronic genius, captivated the audience at the outset. Her voice was full, rich and vibrant; her figure tall and stately. She spoke like an angel and moved like a goddess. Those who saw her predicted a brilliant future for her.

Monday, September 4th, 1876, the theater was formally opened for the fall campaign by Haverly and his minstrels.

The young comedienne Kitty Blanchard and Nellie Cummings, and our Mrs. Germon in the fairy spectacle of the "Naiad Queen." An incident in the performance was the presence in uniform of the Washington Military and their visitors—several crack rifle teams They came by invitation, and added much to the attractions of the theater.

STUART ROBSON.

The first of October saw Stuart Robson for the first time at the National, in Brete Hart's new play written for Robson, entitled, "Two Men of Sandy Bar," with the star as Col. Starbottle.

Both the actor and play met with a warm welcome and commendation from a large and critical audience.

October 16th, Maggie Mitchell as "Fnachon." A week after, Genevieve Rogers as "Maude Muller." Miss Rogers showed herself to be an actress of very fair abilities, never rising to greatness, but never sinking below mediocrity.

BEN. DE BAR.

Mr. Ben DeBar next as "Falstaff." With the memory of the inimitable Hackett fresh in the minds of many of the *habitues* of the National, Mr. DeBar was too heavily handicapped and coldly criticized to make a striking success.

It was evident that the mantle of the dead actor had not fallen upon him. Yet the rendition was undoubtedly a fine one, and in one or two scenes his strong acting brought down the house.

The week after, Mr. G. F. Rowe, in "Brass," an appropriate title that night.

Christmas eve, the Soldene Comic Opera Troupe had good business.

KATE CLAXTON.

Christmas night, Kate Claxton in her great role of the "Two Orphans." Bonnie Kate always started a fire, or the fire followed her wherever she went, in the hotel, taverns, and even a church caught fire when she was praying. So of course, her usual luck followed her. During the snow scene a fight between two hoodlums took place in the gallery, which attracted much notice and caused great commotion, a shout of fight! fight! fight! soon changed in to the fearful cry of fire, and the audience with the memory of the dreadful Brooklyn disaster fresh in their minds, and knowing that Kate Claxton brought fire as naturally as an owl flying in the day time signifies rain, broke for the door. The ushers kept their coolness, threw wide the portals, and then the orchestra struck up a jovial air, which soon brought the panic to an end, and the people returned to their seats, many heartily ashamed of the frenzied endeavors to escape a purely imaginary danger.

THE YEAR OF 1877.

Mary Anderson opened the New Year of 1877 with a two weeks' engagement, her repertoire being "Juliet," "Parthenia," "Pauline," "Lady Macbeth," and "Meg Merriles." Her youthful roles were her strong ones; her vivid freshness and beauty making her the realism of the love lorne and love born maidens, but her Meg Merriles' were an utter failure, and the press condemned it so unmistakably that she never again tried the role. Her "Lady Macbeth" also awoke a storm of criticisms, and she was glad to give that up also.

FRANK BANGS AND AGNES BOOTH.

The greatest spectacular play ever seen at the National was brought on January 22, 1877. It cast into the shade even Kiralfy's "Black Crook," and "Around the World." It was Byron's play of "Sardanapalus," with F. C. Bangs, Agnes Booth, and Louis Aldrich as the attractions. The play was magnificently mounted, and its corps de ballet was immense. For two weeks the theater was filled to its utmost capacity, and it could have run a month longer to full houses.

Boucicault achieved a triumph as Con, in the "Shaugraun." It was a wonderful power that made a rather debilitated man of fifty-four assume the character of a young Irish lad, and carry it off successfully.

Boucicault was such a great favorite with the journalists at large, and newspaper row in particular, that the newspaper men and correspondent formed a club and named it in his honor—"The Shaugraun Club." It was designed to be like the celebrated "Kit-Kat Club" of London, but jealousies and rivalries among the members soon dissolved it.

GALLERY SUPPORT.

John T. Raymond now brings out a new play called, "There's Millions In It," and it drew well, of course.

For six nights John Owens held the boards with the "Heir at Law," "Our Boys" and "Solon Shingle," to only moderate audiences.

HENRY J. MONTAGUE.

The 1st of March witnessed the advent of a young English actor that won an astonishing popularity among the people. He was strikingly like Charles Mathews, only more graceful, and comely, his name was Henry J. Montague, and he gave brilliant promise of being the first comedian of the English stage. He captivated the audiences of the National for a week in a play called "False Shame." Even the critics were won by his natural genial acting and ceased to fire at him those cruel envenomed shafts that had made so many proud actors cower, and which had abated many a haughty crest.

On April 10, E. L. Davenport, in a drama called "Daniel Druce." It did not prove a paying card.

ROBSON AND CRANE.

Those two princes of good fellows, Stuart Robson and William Crane, now dramatically married, and in indissolvable bonds, were as one. They were in sporting parlance a good pair to draw to. They proved themselves the best couple of stars that ever made their bow before the footlights or counted up their heavy cash receipts after the performance. The play "Our Boarding House," now so familiar to the theater goers, was just brought out then, and it was something new and novel, and the old National's walls echoed with roars of genuine merriment.

Another unique innovation and a character, appears before the footlights that was never-seen before; a being that was to furnish in the future much of the funny part of the comedy of the day. The stage had its typical Yankee—with the knife and the stick which he whittled; its stout Dutchman with rotund form and immense pipe; its Southerner with wide slouching hat, pants stuffed in the boots, and the revolver and bowie knife close to the hand; the Irishman with the battered beaver, shillalah under his arm, a pipe between his teeth, and ready to dance or fight, it did not make a difference; but the "Celestial" was thought too devoid of humor to be worth while to work him up. But the genius of Brete Harte it found a rich mine in John Chinamen, and Charles T. Parsloe's rendition of "Ah Sin" showed that the Chinese have as much wit and humor in them as any other nationality. Not only the novelty, but the fine acting of Mr. Parsloe met with a prosperity that amazed even the managers, authors and actors themselves. The Washington press criticisms of this play were very flattering, but for some reason it was shortly afterwards abandoned.

On June 4th the National was closed for the season by the San Francisco Minstrels.

The fall season was commenced by the Park Theater Company in a vapid nonsensical jumble of words called "Baby." The critics riddled it, but the audience were too polite to hiss.

GEORGE S. KNIGHT.

September 10th, George Knight in his German character sketch in a play called "Otto." He was assisted by the Worrell Sisters, and they gave a very enjoyable performance to large houses.

MAUDE GRANGER.

After them came Maude Granger, supported by Louis James, in "Camille." The statuesque Maude made by far the most beautiful Mlle Gautier that the audience had ever seen, for she had a figure that Rubens would have loved to paint—a Byron describe—large, full, sensuous. On a pose in a tableau Miss Granger was a success, but as an actress in such a character as "Camille," she was an insolvent in the dramatic bank, and more people went to see her out of curiosity than with a desire to be entertained.

ANNIE WARREN STORY.

With Miss Florence Carey as the leading lady in the play of the Danicheffs was a young Washington maiden, Miss Annie Story who made her debut as the Princess, and fully satisfied the expectations of her friends. A press criticism says of her;

> The most interesting event of the evening was the debut of Miss Anna Story, who sustained the role of the Princess to the full satisfaction of a critical audience.

Then follows Lydia Thompson with her troupe of blondes, in "Robinson Crusoe," which drew a large crowd, if not a critical audience, yet a very encoring one.

John McCullough, the first week in December, to a brliant audience, in his various roles. He was at his zenith of fame, and the highest in the land always welcomed him. His engagement proved a most profitable one.

LOUISE POMEROY.

Another star of the first magnitude and hailing from Clara Morris' native town, now gave a week's engagement in her Shaksperaean roles. A born tragedienne, a real actress, was Louise Pomeroy, and her Rosalind, in "As You Like It," was the finest ever seen in this country. Tall, graceful, with just such eyes as an actress should have, a wealth of yellow hair, and superb voice, she made a great success. Her playing was slightly marred by mannerism, which a longer practice would cure. Her dramatic powers were acknowledged by the press as being of the highest order, and her success was such that she was engaged at a high figure for a southern tour. Miss Annie Story accompanied her.

Then Joe Jefferson, as the ever welcome "Rip Van Winkle."

Aimee sparkled for a week in the Opera Bouffe, which ended the year of '77.

THE YEAR OF 1878.—LAWRENCE BARRETT.

A fine opening in January was made by Lawrence Barrett, in "Richelieu" and "Hamlet."

Miss Kellogg and Annie Louise Carey, in Italian and English Opera, to enormous houses.

January 21, Miss Maggie Moore and Mr. J. C. Williamson in a play called, "Struck Oil." They did not strike it—at least not in the National.

Sothern in the "Crushed Tragedian," amused and delighted the city for a week. No man on earth but Sothern could make anything of the "Crushed," but in his hands it was inimitable, and to him it was a veritable bonanza.

MADAME MOJESKA.

Madame Mojeska now appears to subdue and charm, and her "Camille" was the wonder of the times; not so emotional as others before her, but for consummate acting, exquisite grace, and marvellous truth to nature, she was matchless; and the critics, the audience and playrights praised her acting as simply imcomparable. One of the morning papers thus speaks of her:

Taller than Mary Anderson, with a lithe and slender form, her every movement and pose is easy, graceful, and artistic. Her voice is clear, delightfully modulated, so that without acting it would faithfully express the varied emotions which, by the perfection of the art, seem real and not simulated. There are some who, notwithstanding the New York critics, will still prefer the 'Camille' of Clara Morris, but it is unfair to compare these two great artists at all, as their methods are so essentially different.

During the months of February, March and April, 1878, the old favorites of the theater—Maggie Mitchell, Dion Boucicault, John T. Raymond, Lotta, Fanny Davenport, John McCullough—appeared respectively. Carncross' Minstrels in May, and in June, J. Remington Fairlamb, in "Valerie."

JOHN W. ALBAUGH, MANAGER.

The season opens September 2, 1878, with Mr. Albaugh of the Holliday street Theatre, Baltimore, as lessee and manager.

SAMUEL G. KINSLEY

This season opens September 2, 1878, with John W. Albaugh as lessee and manager, and Samuel G. Kinsley as business manager. Mr. Albaugh acting as general supervisor over both of his theaters in Baltimore and Washington, and Mr. Kinsley devoting all of his time to the National.

Samuel G. Kinsley now appears on the scene as connected with the theater, and his name is henceforth linked with the National, and for nearly a decade of years its great success, next to the enterprise of its owner, Mr. Rapley, is due to his untiring energy, rare forethought and delicate tact which meets and conquers all difficulties. As the business manager is the soul of the newspaper, so is he the mainspring of the theatrical clock, and to his finely tempered qualities more than any other cause is due the great prosperity and popularity of the theater.

Samuel G. Kinsley started his theatrical life as the advance agent for Edwin Forrest. Then he filled the same position for John S. Clarke, Lydia Thompson, the great Hermann and the beautiful Adelaide Neilson. He was next business manager of the famous Lucille Western, and he made her a winning card by his finesse. Then he took E. A. Sothern and managed so as to make him the rage. Next Mr. Joe Jefferson engaged him, and placed his future in his hands, leaving all the details to him, and only following his guidance.

Under Mr. Kinsley's care these artists realized handsome fortunes.

All the ripe judgment and trained experience that Mr Kinsley had gained by years of hard work was brought to bear, and so on the public saw that the business of the National was to be conducted on an enduring basis, and not as a make shift for a season by a manager who would probably be forced to throw up his contract at the end of the year.

But it is the personal character of the man that has impressed the citizens of Washington so strongly for his honesty, truthfulness and trustworthiness that has had much to do with the success of the theater, and he has conquered that mysterious unseen power called public opinion which makes or mars many a public enterprise.

The attraction the first night was Duprez and Benedict's Minstrels.

W. F. CODY.

They were succeeded by the Minzelle Sisters, in the "Ice Witch," and in turn followed by W. F. Cody, in a blood and thunder border play called "Lost and Won," in which the typical Forty-Niner uttered heroic sentiments, that caused the young girls to applaud, and kept up a lively fusillade with the revolver, killing bandits and Indians at every fire, and made the gallery gods hoarse with yells of delight.

Mr. F. C. Bangs, rises from his staturesque pose of "Sardanapalus," and tries the role of Philip Falconbridge, in "King John" He was a better voluptuous Assyrian than the bold rollicking Britain. He was too heavy for the part, yet at times he rose far above mediocrity.

EMMA ABBOTT.

September 30, John E. Owens, in "Our Boys," October 1st, Mrs. Southworth's novel dramatized called the "Hidden Hand," by a local stock company. October 1878, Emma Abbott for the first time at the National with the Hess English Opera Company, which was designed to replace Kellogg.

HISTORY OF THE NEW NATIONAL THEATER. 77

Robert Heller, the magician, in a week's engagement.

November 28th, Kiralfy Brothers in their grand spectacular exhibition of Jules Verne's novel, "A Trip to the Moon." It was a magnificent display and well patronized, as it deserved to be.

Little Miss Lotta played her pranks for a week in a new comedy written for her called "La Cigale." Of course she drew well. Lotta and a crowded house was a natural sequence. If she was advertised to play alone, she could draw a large audience and charm them, simply by the aid of musicians, girlish, gladsome gaiety, her jovial banjo, and a captivating song or two.

Christmas week was a superb bill of fare. One that would cater to the taste of the most fastidious dramatic gourmand. Kellogg returns to the National, bringing with her Anna Louise Cary, and the famous Italian songstress, Mlle. Litta. For a week these artists held the vast audiences enthralled by their glorious voices. Mignon was the favorite opera, as all three took part in it, and the old National rarely witnessed more real enthusiasm over real art.

And what discordant discord is that which follows the divine tones of the chantresses, why it is Haverly's Horse Opera. The heavenly cadence of Litta's voice in *Con nais tu le pays* has already ceased to echo through the edifice; that it is broken by a rasping howl of a negro minstrel shouting "Whoa, Emma."

THE YEAR OF 1879.

The empress of her art, Helena Modjeska, with her whole repertoire of "Camille," "Frou Frou," "East Lynne," "Adriene," and "Juliet," for two weeks, from the middle of January to February. Beauty, fashion and money gathered to hear her, and night after night she charmed every one by her superb renditions. There was no sameness in her acting; every emotion had its glance and gestures, and she could have been understood when playing before a deaf and dumb asylum.

Lawrence Barrett again in heroic roles supported by the talented young actor, T. W. Keene. McKee Rankin and Kitty Blanchard made a great hit with their new play, "The Danites." Everybody thronged to see it, and the box office showed fat receipts.

Not so with Mr. B. McCauley, as "Uncle Daniel." A reaction took place, and the tide went out and the theater goers paid a penance of several weeks for their untoward dissipation during the winter, when the stars trod the boards.

Denman Thompson, as "Joshua Witcomb." Dion Boucicault as Conn, in "The Shaughraun." The dramatic tide rose again to its flood when Robson and Crane gave the "Comedy of Errors."

Joe Jefferson, as "Rip," and fighting "Bob Acres," attracted the usual multitude.

On April 16, the city went wild over a new opera of Gilbert and Sullivan, it was the immortal "Pinafore." There was never in the annals of the stage such a wonderful and marvellous success, since Gay's great production of the "Beggars Opera" took London by storm, and made Rich, the manager of the Old Drury Lane Theater, one of the wealthiest men in England. George Selwin wittily observed that the "Beggars Opera" made Gay-Rich, and Rich-Gay.

"Pinafore" was music that the public could understand and enjoy; the music sparkled, laughed and flashed and exhilarated one like a deep draught of Roderer wine. It was the opera by the people, for the people, of the people, and they claimed it and adopted "Pinafore" as theirs. It knew no section, from cultivated New England to the wild west and far south, it was heard, caught up, and appropriated. Everybody went, and Pinafore troupes were going through every hamlet and cross-roads of the land reaping rich harvests. At a New York theater it run for one hundred nights without a break to crowded houses. One touch of melody makes the world akin, and it was the one opera where all met on equal ground, and the clapping of the kid gloves that covered slender hands, the thump of the claquer's stick, and the shrill yelp of the gallery gods, all mingled together in a heavily and spontaneous tribute to the music of "Pinafore."

English opera gave way to the Italian, and Emma Abbott with Hess Company gave a week of very enjoyable entertainment.

Here comes the ladies and gentlemen of color, the sons and daughters of Africa, in "Pinafore." They did quite well.

The National was opened for the fall season on September 15, 1879, by the greatest of all magicians "the one, the only Hermann," who performed such astounding legerdemain as to make many of his auditors believe that he was really in league with the devil.

Next the fair Adah Richmond and her Comic Opera Company in "Fatinitza," to such an audience as a player loves to look upon.

Mr. and Mrs. John W. Albaugh in "Van, the Virginian," followed by Rice's Surprise Party, which was succeeded in time by The Tourists in the Pullman Palace Car.

Mr. and Mrs. Florence in the "Mighty Dollar." Maggie Mitchell in her roles. Henry Sargeant in "Contempt of Court." Emma Abbott again. John McCullough and his repertoire of heroic plays. McKee Rankin in the "Danites," The popular "Pinafore" again, this time by the best troupe on the road—"Haverly's Chicago Church Choir Co." Rice's Combination in "Evangeline." Christmas week, Kate Claxton in the "Double Marriage," and the "Two Orphans."

THE YEAR OF 1880.

Mr. Sothern opened the new year by his *piece de resistance* of the "American Cousin."

January 19, Lotta, in "Musette," and the "Little Detective."

On the 26th, Miss Fanny Davenport, for a week, in "Pique," "As You Like It," and "Cymbeline," to poor business.

Joe Emmett followed in "Fritz in Ireland," that proved very popular.

"Fun on the Bristol," by Henry Jarrett's company did not pan out well in this city.

Miss Ada Cavendish for a week in Shakespearean roles.

"The Tourists," again, followed by Miss Mary Anderson, who scored a triumph in her "Evadne."

Oliver Doud Byron, in "Across the Continent," and Louis Aldrich, in "My Partner," to moderate houses.

"The Bankers Daughter," a new play, met with success.

Lawrence Barrett, for a week, in "Richelieu," "David Garrick," and "Hamlet."

April 12, Carncross Minstrels.

April 19, Emma Abbott and her Opera Company. She was followed by Maurice Grau's French Opera Company, which played to a theater well filled.

"Rices' Surprise Party" for the fourth time, and then Miss Annie Graham, a novice, in a play called "Upper Crust," to a scant audience.

It will be noticed that a good many unknown actresses appear in a theater and then disappear, and are heard of no more. Few know of the amount of steady, persistent labor it requires to make even a respectable actress. A young woman who has the art of mimicry and some talent, imagines she is a born artist. She provides herself with a gorgeous wardrobe, places herself in the hands of an agent, gives money freely, takes a few lessons in elocution that invariably gives her a stilted declamatory and artificial style; learns her part, and then rushes on the boards to find disappointment and wounded feelings, and mortified **vanity**.

Madam Mars was the "Louise de Liquerolles of Legouve," yet, before the curtain of the Theater Francais rose upon the piece, she had had *sixty-eight rehearsals*. Fanny Kemble wore a court costume and train in her house for a whole year so as to get accustomed to it. Ristori studied the part of "Marie Antoinette" three years before she dared to act it before the footlights. The great Rachael retired to her country seat and remained three months alone, to study the last act of "Adrienne Lecouvre." All the great stars only won their proud eminence by intense and long continued work.

The close of the summer season was marked by Abbey's Comic Opera Company, in "Humpty Dumpty."

September 13, Jarrett's Opera Company, with "Cinderella or the Little Glass Slipper." "A Golden Game," by Shannon and Edeson to a thin audience. Hermann, the Magician, followed "The Tourists." Next Maggie Mitchell, then Rice's Surprise Company, and lastly by Maude Granger, in "Two Nights in Rome."

November 8, E. E. Rice's Bijou Comic Opera Company, in the "Spectre Knight."

Miss Ada Cavendish, in a play, below mediocrity, called "The Soul of an Actress."

"The Pirates of Penzance," made the first hit of the season, and an old time crowd filled the National.

Lotta again, and as the little actress peeped through the curtain just before its rise, she had no cause to complain of a thin house.

December 13, Chanfrau, in "Kit," to a good business.

Christmas week, Kiralfy Bros., in the spectacular drama of "Around the World in Eighty Days," to an immense audience.

The old year died when Robson and Crane were holding the boards, in "Sharps and Flats."

A singular incident occured at this theater at one of the engagements of these favorites—Robson and Crane. A drunken man went to the National to see "Sharps and Flats." This son of Bacchus paid his twenty-five cents, climbed the steps to the pea nut gallery, gave his ticket to the doorkeeper, ambled in and found a seat in an obscure corner, and, lulled by the strains of the orchestra, dropped into a profound slumber. The roars of laughter at Robson's falsetto and Crane's deep baritone only served to stir phantasies in his brain, and after the curtain fell, the noise of the audience leaving the house, only lulled him into deeper sleep. The doors were locked and black darkness took the place of the dazzling light, and away after midnight the imbiber of mixed and straight drinks awoke with a consuming thirst and parched tongue, and in his soddened brain their flashed no idea of who he was, or where he was, his only thought was that he must have a drink; so impelled, he got up and stumbled around loose; he reached the enclosure of the gallery, climbed over it and fell headlong from the fourth tier clear down to the pit.

There is an old and true saying which saith that a special Providence watches over sailors, children and drunken men. Any sober person would have been killed outright or horribly mangled, but this son of inebriety, though he fell without a break, and smashed four of the orchestra chairs to kindling wood, yet did not get a bruise. He scrambled up, got out of a window, and the next morning came back looking for his hat.

THE YEAR OF 1881.

Kate Claxton opened the new year with a play called the "Snow Flower."

John McCullough next in his old repertoire.

January 24, Emmett in "Fritz," succeeded by Mary Anderson in her favorite roles. As she passed off the stage Joe Jefferson came on with his two best characters, "Rip" and "Bob Acres."

February 14, Nat C. Goodwin in "Hobbies."

A week of music with Emma Abbott in the various operas.

Lawrence Barrett in his old plays, and the Pullman Car Tourists by the New York Stock Company. Carncross and Dixies' Minstrels followed.

SARAH BERNHARDT.

Friday, April 8th, was the event of the season, and the public who had heard of the fame of Sarah Bernhardt, now had a chance to see the most famous actress on the globe.

This great artist, like Rachæl, had climbed to the top from the very bottom, and she had only herself to thank for her success. In Paris she struggled for years to obtain the merest pit'ance to keep body and soul together, and at times she was so poverty-stricken, so ill used, so unappreciated, that she meditated suicide, and once actually took several ounces of laudanum, and her life was saved only by the prompt treatment of a physician. She frequently declared that she suffered a hundred deaths before fame and fortune came to her. Yet she struggled on, animated with the knowledge that she had talent, and the world must sooner or later acknowledge it. At last, like the immortal Siddons, her transcendent genius burst through the dark clouds in a blinding flash, and in a few brief weeks the scorned stock actress stood acknowledged as the one on whom the mantle of Rachæl had fallen. All Paris bowed in homage before her, and in the supreme hour of triumph with the emotional Parisians at her feet, all of hardships must have been atoned for.

After conquering Europe she came to the New World, and her progress was like that of a victorious Roman general with his banner blazoned with: "Io Triumphe."

When the curtain drew up in the play of "Frou Frou," all eyes watched intently for her coming, and they saw a lithesome figure glide upon the stage with the grace of a leopard, the soft indescribable undulative motion was so peculiarly her own, that it was never witnessed on the boards before. But her acting was the most perfect of the French school, which is the most perfect in the world. Her actions, gestures and glances were the perfection of histrionic power, blending the emotional strength of tragic art. More melo-dramatic, more passionate style has been witnessed on the stage of the National Theater; but never such consummate acting. As powerful as was her rendition in "Frou Fiou," it was not until she played "Camille," that her matchless talents displayed itself. Her life, so much like that unfortunate woman's, her temptations, her trials in the same city among the same people so identified her with the part, that she was literally "Camille" herself. Her acting was subdued, yet effective and not until the climax was reached did the stormy power that lay hid in that slight frame burst out, then, indeed, did she ascend to the very zenith of passion. The death scene while not so powerful as other stars, yet was incomparably more realistic acting. It was a death bed scene, but a peaceful one, that came as a welcome relief to a long suffering woman and not the torturing struggling death that overtook her as a retribution.

A press notice says of her appearance at the National:

The audience last night at the National Theater, despite the treble prices, was not only immense, but was of the highest quality, almost everybody of prominence in society, or public or professional life was there. Many were there who had not been in the theater for years. Madame Bernhardt won more and more upon her audience, and she was called out by the wildly enthusiastic people again and again.

April 11, John T. Raymond, in a new play called "Fresh, the American." The verdict of the Washington public was against this comedy, it had rather too much Raymond in it.

The Acme Olivette Company to crowded houses. This new opera was a success from the jump. It had many of the old Washington favorites in it. Carleton of the Ritching's and Kellogg Troupe; H. C. Peakes and Fanny Wentworth.

R. G. INGERSOLL.

Sunday, May 8, Bob Ingersoll delivered his lecture called "The Great Infidel and the Devil." While the famous Free Thinker advocated pulling down the old creeds, he did not say or hint what he would erect in their places. This lecture closed the theater for the season with a strong smell of brimstone in the air.

The National, newly papered, painted and frescoed was opened September 8, 1881, by Barlow and Wilson's burnt cork artists.

Miss Jennie Lee, next, as Joe, in "Bleak House," to an exceedingly small audience.

Miss Alice Harrison, in "Photos," to a few listless people.

Mr. and Mrs. Knight, in "Baron Rudolph," to a small but attentive audience.

Sam Hague's British Operatic Minstrels must have thought the cholera or some kind of pestilence was raging in Washington judging from the funeral solemnity that rested on the faces of about a score of people who sat scattered about almost lost in the vast depth of the building

But Kiralfy and brother brought the crowd with their splendid spectacular play of Michael Strogoff.

October 17, Mr. and Mrs Goodwin in "Camille; or, the Cracked Heart," and thereby hangs a tale. They had heavily billed the city, and their posters were gorgeous affairs. Business is business, and the proprietors of a new glue who were just starting a patent sticking fluid on the market, pasted their placards under the cracked hearts, with the words: "Let Camille use Blank's prepared glue."

THOMAS W. KEENE.

The next week Mr. Thos. W. Keene in Shakespearean plays.

Emma Abbott follows with her opera company.

Hermann with his latest sensation "The Automaton Wonders," to a good sized audience.

Mr and Mrs. Florence in their specialties.

Mary Anderson, much improved every way, now gave a series of renditions of "Juliet," "Parthenia," "Evadne," and the "Lady of Lyons."

Fanny Davenport followed her in Shakespearean heroines.

Pretty, piquant Miss Lotta as "Bob," by far her best character.

The Vokes Family gave a week's enjoyable entertainment with their plays, the "Belles of the Kitchen," "Joe," and "Fun in a Fog."

THE YEAR OF 1882.

January 2d, "Joshua Whitcomb," by Mr. Denman Thompson.

Robson and Crane came next with "Our Bachelors," and "Sharps and Flats."

Lawrence Barrett in his old roles.

January 23d, Colville's sensational spectacular drama, "The World."

John McCullough, and Joe Emmett to large houses in their respective parts.

February 24th, the Grand Italian Opera for three nights, "Carmen," "Aida," and "Lohengrin," given to large and fashionable audiences.

The genial John Raymond follows in "Fresh," and the inimitable "Col. Mulberry Sellers."

Maggie Mitchell next in the "Little Savage."

Joe Jefferson in his two roles that people never seemed to tire of.

ADA GRAY.

April 24, for a week, Miss Ada Gray in "East Lynne." Her engagement was an utter failure; there were not fifty people in the house, and those not of the melting kind. They sat as glum as if they were at a funeral waiting for the corpse to be brought in.

May 8, Miss Emily Rigl made a hit in the play of "Her Atonement."

MARGARET LARNER AND R. L. DOWNING.

Miss Margaret Larner, assisted by R. L. Downing, in the "Princess of Bagdad."

No young actor has attained a more enviable reputation than Mr. Downing. Commencing at the very foot of the ladder he has by earnest and persevering work reached a round where the top is in sight. For years he struggled hard in subordinate positions, but finally in the support of Mary Anderson he had an opportunity to develop the ability that was in him, and his Ingomar, Huon and Cololona compared favorably with the greatest of his predecessors. His seasons with Joe Jefferson gave him an experience in comedy, and his Captain Absolute and John Perrybingle were successful efforts. If his development fulfils the promise of his early career it will not be many years before R. L. Downing will fill the void in the roll of tragedians made by the retirement of John McCullough.

There have been given on the boards of the National many amateur operas, the performances having always been presented for some worthy charity. Among the operas thus produced may be mentioned "Martha," "Pinafore," "Pirates of Penzance," and "Cox and Box," but perhaps the most notable was the "Chimes of Normandy," which was performed by the following cast:

THE CHIMES OF NORMANDY.
May 29, 1882. BENEFIT OF SAMUEL G. KINSLEY.

Serolette	Miss Eva Mills
Germaine	Mrs. E. B. True
Manette	Mrs. Hamilton Adams
Jeannie	Mrs. D. McLeod
Gertrude	Mrs. J. W. Cross
Susannah	Miss Iola Williams
Henri	Mr. John Pugh
Robert More	Mr. J. F. Rule
Gaspard	Mr. E. B. Hay
Bailliff	Mr. Lewis Seibold
Notary	Mr. H. A. Forsman
Attendants	Mr. E. H. Clifford / " C. Donahue

Barlow and Wilson's Minstrels opened the autumn campaign of September 4, 1882.

McKee Rankin, followed by a play called "49."

Bartley Campbell's "Galley Slave," was brought out for the first time by a New York Company, and scored an unqualified success.

Kiralfy Bros. to jammed houses and enthusiastic audiences with the old but welcome "Black Crook." It showed that the Washington people never get tired of a spectacular play when well mounted and with a fine "corps de ballet." It is only the cheap imitations they kick so against.

October 9, Bartley Campbell's "White Slave," to a fine and applauding audience.

Collier's "Lights O' London," did a rushing business for a week.

Brooks and Dickson's Dramatic Company, in "The World," followed by N. C. Goodwin and E. F. Thorne, in the "Black Flag."

The great tragedienne Modjeska, again trod the boards of the National, in "As You Like It," and "Frou Frou." The society people turned out *en masse*, and she furnished a topic of conversation among the *haut ton* for a nine days period.

Joe Jefferson, as "Rip" and "Bob."

Then Thomas W. Keene, in "Richard" and "Hamlet," who played during the Christmas holidays to good houses.

THE YEAR OF 1883.

Miss Mary Anderson opened the new year with her various roles. Her success was acknowledged by every one of the theater habitues, and a Washington audience is certainly the coolest, most fastidious one in the Union, like Iago they are "nothing, if not critical."

Little Miss Lotta, again das "Bob," in breeches.

January 15, Robson an Crane, in a laughable play called "Forbidden Fruits."

February 26, Lawrence Barrett appeared with a new tragedy, by Hon. George Boker, called "Francesca da Rimini," a realization of Dante's celebrated story. Barrett had played in the National for years in various heroic roles, with distinguished success, but on that February night the Washington play goers were destined to be astonished, as they were never astonished before. The troupe supporting Barrett was an exceptionally strong one. F. C. Moseby took the part of Guido Da Polenta, the head of the Ghebelins; Louis James, as Pepe, the Jester; B. G. Rogers, as Malatestan, Lord of Rimini; Francesca, by the beautiful Marie Wainwright, and Ritta, by Ada Plunkett.

The acting of Barrett was natural and easy in the two first acts; he rose in passion in the third, but in the fourth scene, in the interior of the celebrated Cathedral at Rimini, when the marriage of Guido's daughter takes place, he ascended to the very acme of passionate acting. He was superb. Such intensity, such rage, horror and hatred; such delineation of a storm tossed soul, the stage of the old theater never witnessed before. The audience were amazed. Could that be Barrett? Impossible. In the last act and scene he was appalling, when he came into the chamber armed with the dagger, disordered in mind, driven on to seek a blind vengeance for treachery that the gods themselves could not pardon; he was a ghastly spectacle; his complexion pallid, his voice inarticulate, his eyes like burning coals of fire. He stops short, irresolute; his countenance changes, then over the face steals the horrible repulsive remembrance; it hardens, becomes fixed; the rigid hand clutches the poniard, the other seeks the heart and trembles at finding it, for the memory of many years rushes over him and rises like a veil of tears between his vengeance and the woman he loved. The right pla had found the right man at last, and the tumultuous applause showed Barrett that he had attained the proud position of one of the greatest tragedians that the new world had ever produced. Among the great debuts of great actors, his can be counted, and "Da Rimini," will always hereafter be inseparably connected with the name of Lawrence Barrett.

Barrett's great faculties have in this play full sway; he renders hate so terribly, irony so frightfully, disdain so contemptuously, devotion so entrancing, love so inexpressibly sweet; while the whole house rivet their eyes, hold their breath, as their hearts throb under the mystic influence. Francesca, the daughter of Guido, Lord of Ravenna, was given by her father in marriage to Lanciotto, Lord of Rimini, a man hideously deformed. Afraid of disgusting his bride, Lanciotto resolved to woo by proxy, and sent as his representative his brother Paolo, who was the handsomest and most accomplished cavalier in Italy. He won the bride's heart, and, forgetful of his brother's trust ruined her, and Lanciotta finding out the betrayal, in his maddening rage, put both of them to death.

Madame Janauschek follows as "Marie Antoinette."

April 2, John T. Raymond in a new play called "In Paradise." It was a weak production, and the press damned it with faint praise.

Maggie Mitchell again in same old roles.

April 16, Miss Catherine Lewis caused a sensation, altogether of a pleasant kind, in "Olivette," and she proved one of the best paying cards of the season.

Hermann with his diabolistic tricks came after her.

The season was closed by a regular rousing outpouring of Mr. Sam Kinsley's numerous friends who attended his benefit, the Washington Operatic Association giving "Pinafore" in unsurpassed style, with Miss Eva Mills as Josephine.

The minstrels as usual opened the fall season.

September 10, 1883, "East Lynne" again.

Mr. John Jack as "King Henry the Fourth." If the English monarch looked and acted like Mr. Jack, it is no wonder his subjects rebelled.

Miss Kate Claxton follows in the "Sea of Ice."

October 1, Bartley Campbell's play of "Siberia," was brought out in fine style, and has become the most popular of all his productions.

The Hess Opera Company next. Miss Abbie Carrington made a most favorable impression in the role of "Martha."

The "Romany Rye" did a large business for a week, and they were followed by the "Silver King" to small houses.

Raymond and Maggie Mitchell in their respective parts.

December 10, Lawrence Barrett to a "crush" in "Da Rimini."

Mr. James O'Neil came after in "Monte Cristo."

"In the Ranks," by a travelling company, was presented, finely mounted, and well played, and met with deserved success.

THE YEAR OF 1884.

Joe Jefferson in his old roles. He gave one rendition of Caleb Plummer, in the "Cricket on the Hearth," which many think is his strongest character. Full audiences greeted him.

Jan. 21, 1884, John McCaul's Opera Company, in the "Queen's Lace Handkerchief." The music of this production is light and frothy- the scores poor and ineffective. The business was light and the audience critical and undemonstrating.

Mr. and Mrs. Florence in their old characters.

Mr. John McCullough now makes his last appearance on the boards of the National Theater, which he has graced so long. His friends were shocked at the change a few months had made. His great vitality had left him, his fire was dimmed, his passion subdued, and he played aimlessly. His Virginius was a pitiable exhibition of his failing powers. He was a wreck, but a magnificent one still. As the curtain fell on the night of the 24th of February, 1884, upon the battle scene of "Richard the Third," many of the audience thought then that they were taking their last look at him.

Poor John McCullough—a born actor—a good friend and princely gentleman. His loss will long be felt; his epitaph should be like that of Sir Launcelot of Greeves.

John McCullough probably enjoyed more personal popularity than any acter who ever trod the American stage. Genial in disposition, easy and affable in manner, he had a wealth of good fellowship, which made him a most delightful companion, and won the esteem of all with whom he came in contact. Without genius but with great talent, and possessing the advantages of a classi-

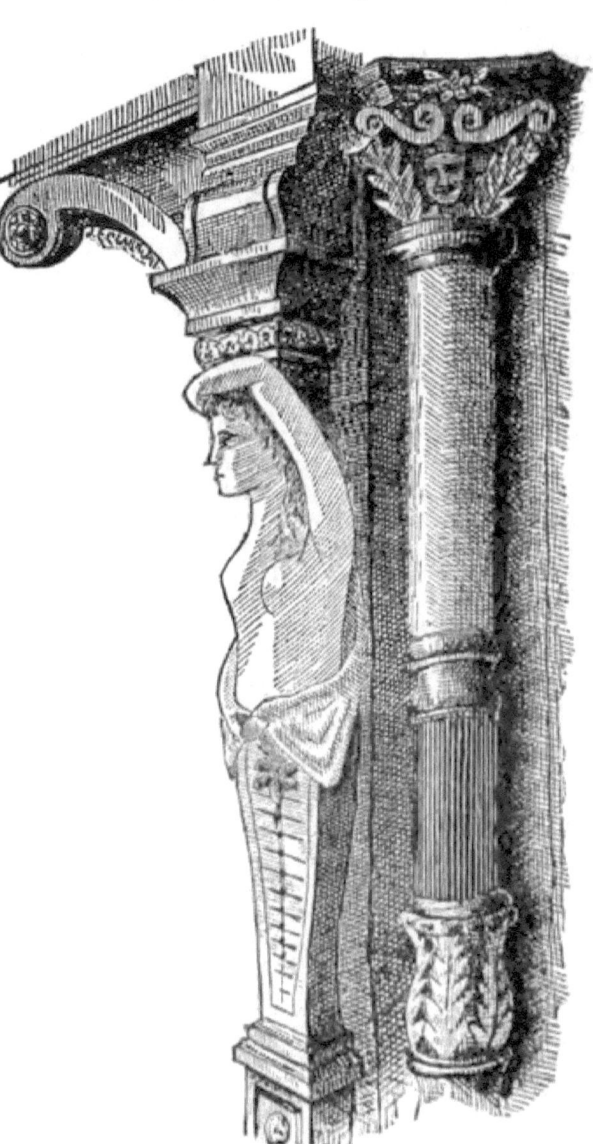

PRIVATE BOX DECORATION.

cal face and magnificent physique, his acting, though traditional and imitative, being modeled on that of his precepter Edwin Forrest, was conscientious and earnest, and his splendid stage presence was sufficient compensation to the masses for his deficient mentality. No critic wished to say harsh things about John, for he was such a jolly good fellow; and it was only when his defects were painfully apparent, as in "Hamlet;" that he received anything but the kindest treatment. Poor John, noble, manly, generous to a fault, his present unfortunate condition is due to his superabundance of animal spirits and his excessive good fellowship.

It so happened that the first publication of the mental impairment of McCullough was made by the writer in a daily newspaper in this city. Immediately there came an emphatic denial from his manager, which was published, and it was hoped that the information received as to the tragedian's condition was incorrect.

But when the actor visited this city the next winter, the truth of his mental decadence was evident to all. The writer visited him in his dressing room and was shocked at the great change in the man. He appeared moody and preoccupied, and repeated himself over and over again in conversation. Once he tried to brighten up and be his old self, but the attempt was a dismal failure and the expression of his face settled back into the dull, leaden, far away look it had worn before. As I came out to the front of the theater I said to his agent: "That man will never play another season. It is a crime to let him play now."

His present sad state is sincerely regretted, not only by those who knew him personally and who loved him, but by thousands who only were acquainted with him over the footlights. With shattered intellect, and with his glorious form enfeebled and shrunk, the time is not far distant when he must shuffle off this mortal coil and go to "that bourne from whence no traveler returns."

The following is the cast of the last performance of McCullough in this city.

NATIONAL THEATER.

The eminent Tragedian Mr.
JOHN McCULLOUGH,
Supported by a Powerful Company. under the Management of
WM. M CONNER.
Saturday evening. February 24. Shakespeare's Tragedy. in 5 Acts. entitled
RICHARD III.

DUKE OF GLOSTER, afterwards King Richard III	JOHN McCULLOUGH
Richmond	Joseph Haworth
Henry IV	H. A. Langdon
Buckingham	Mark Price
Prince of Wales	Frank Little
Duke of York	Frank Thropp
Catsby	H. C. Barton
Stenley	J. H. Shewell
Tressel	E. Stuart
Norfolk	Edward Spencer
Radcliff	John Dailey
Lieut. of the Tower	Edward Goodwin
Lord Mayor	Edward Wilson
Tyrrel	William Haworth
Oxford	Robert Prichard
Blount	H. S. Thorpe
Officer	Wm. Bower
Queen Elizabeth	Mrs. Augusta Foster
Lady Anna	Miss Viola Allen
Duchess of York	Mrs. C. L. Allen

No wait between Acts II. and III. and Acts IV. and V. The audience will please remain seated and avoid an interruption of the performance.

February 26, Mr. Henry Abbey's Italian Opera Company to crowded houses.

HENRY IRVING AND MISS ELLEN TERRY.

On the first of March the great English actor Henry Irving, with Miss Ellen Terry, stepped before the footlights and faced an audience any actor on earth would be proud to meet. The play was "Louis XI.," and Irving's peculiar mannerism, while it dimmed his great talent, yet could not obscure it. But for Miss Ellen Terry, there were not words strong enough to express the pleasure and satisfaction that her exquisite acting gave. Her Ophelia and Portia were incomparable, and the enthusiasm so long corked up by witnessing indifferent plays, now burst out in rapturous applause at her splendid renditions.

Their engagement was a great success; their receipts were princely.

Maude Granger followed in a play called "Claire and the Forge Master." As far as an exhibition of expensive toilettes worn by Miss Maude were concerned, the play was a success. Only a few people were brave enough to sit the drama out.

March 14, Emmett in his favorite characters.

Dion Boucicault in his threadbare play, "The Shaugraun," followed by M. B Curtis as "Sam'l of Posen."

Edwin Thorne in the blood curdling and crimson current chilling play of "**The Black Flag.**"

April 21, Emma Abbott's Opera Company, in which Signor Tagliapetra scored a great success.

RAPLEY AND KINSLEY, MANAGERS.

The National opened September 8, with Rapley and Kinsley, lessees and managers. Thatcher, Primrose and West's Minstrels led off the ball, followed by Miss Lizzie May Ulmer, Mr. Frank Mayo, Janauschek, M'lle Aimee respectively, in their usual roles, with no new features.

Shook and Collier combination on November 3, in "Storm Beaten."

Then came the Milan Opera Company, with all good artists.

November 17, the Madison Square Company, in Conway's play of "Called Back," to a big business.

Agnes Booth next, in the "**Wages of Sin.**"

"**The Shadows of a Great City**," proved a strong card and drew fine audiences.

Joe Jefferson for the hundredth time in same ancient characters.

"The Pavements of Paris," to small houses.

Christmas week, "The Private Secretary," to a huge audience. This play was a pronounced success from the start and grew steadily in popular favor.

The end of the old year, "**Young Mrs. Winthrop.**"

THE YEAR OF 1885.

The opening of 1885, was marked by **Florence**, in his "Mighty Dollar."

January 12, the beautiful and accomplished M'lle Rhea, in an engagement to standing room only, the play was Howard Carroll's "American Countess."

"May Blossom" by the Madison Square Company to very **poor** houses.

A real sensation was Mestayer's "We, Us & Co." a jumble of odds and ends, yet irresistibly funny, and drew the people to the theater in crowds.

February 2, Fanny Davenport as "Fedora."

February 9, Louis Aldrich in "My Partner" to a few small houses.

On Thursday, January 19, "The Elks," a Washington organization, had a benefit at the theater in which the city St. Cecelia Quartette took part.

The last play that was performed on the boards of the old National was "Victor Durand," by Wallack's New York Company. About three hours after the end of the performance, February 27, 1885, the National caught fire from some unexplained cause and was soon in ruins.

A most striking and wonderful coincidence about those disasters, was the fact that each destruction of the theater occurred just about, or a little previous, to the time of the inauguration of a President, namely: Polk, Buchanan, Grant and Cleveland, in the years 1845, 1857, 1873, and 1885.

The Victor Durand Company lost all of their wardrobe. Agnes Elliott's was valued at $2,500; Louise Dillon's $1,000; M. Gothold's $500; Rollin Buckstone's, $1,500; and Mr. Brunestein's, the manager of the company, at least $12,000.

Mr. Rapley's actual loss was many thousands of dollars, and the prospective damage cannot well be estimated in dollars and cents. Just at the busiest season of the year, and at a time when the installation of a new President brought tens of thousands of strangers to the city that would have jammed his theater and paid royal dividends, he lost his theater; and as he stood at the smoldering ruins he must have felt like giving up in utter despair. But the same feeling that nerved Stanley to penetrate through the dark continent, and Swain to force his way across the Isthmus of Darian, impelled Mr. Rapley, for the second time, to rebuild the theater, and to take a bond of fate.

He deserves the sincere thanks and cordial recognition of the citizens of the capitol city, and he will receive them unstinted, and a most liberal patronage.

CHAPTER VII.

DESCRIPTION OF THE NEW THEATER.

The New National is one of the finest buildings in the Union. All that mechanics and the arts could furnish have been lavishly used, and Mr. W. W. Rapley can gaze with a lofty feeling of pride upon the completion of his work.

The devices for the safety of the audience in any conceivable emergency are so complete that no accident could happen.

The building was commenced on the last day of April, 1885, because May 1st fell on Friday, and there is no man, be he Guelph or Gueberline, who would not prefer to start in a new enterprise, or depart on a long voyage on any other time in the week but hangman's day.

By the first of September the builders finished their portion of the work, and then the decoraters took a hand, and in five weeks the interior was completed.

The entrance to the dress circle is twenty-eight feet wide, and is reached through the lobby, handsomely and tastefully decorated.

The size of the auditoriums are 16 by 80, and will seat fully nineteen hundred people. Before and behind the scenes is divided by an asbestos fire proof stage curtain that would effectually, in a case of fire, prevent its spread towards the front of the house.

The lobby is tiled with alternate diamonds of white and black marble, on each side of which are ladies' and gentlemen's waiting rooms, where refreshments are served in the best style.

The lobby is separated from the theater by massive mahogany folding doors. The stage is both spacious, wide and deep, and as the floor rises with a strong elevation rearward, the view to the stage is perfect from all parts of the house. The chairs in the house are twenty-one inches between the arms. Thus giving an easy seat even to a two hundred and fifty pounds avoirdupois; there is wide spaces between the rows so that the late comer will not cause inconvenience. The floor of the orchestra is laid with heavy Wilton carpet.

The theater is brilliantly lighted. A splendid chandelier, hanging from the center of the roof, contains one hundred burners, with attachments for lighting by electricity, and also for incandescent lights.

The green room is fourteen feet square and superbly furnished. There are twenty-four dressing rooms beside a large trunk room for baggage. There are three rooms for the stars, eleven feet square.

The whole interior of the theater is finished in bright cherry, embossed with gilt, and the ceiling elegantly and tastefully frescoed

The building is heated with steam throughout.

The theater in its appurtenances cost a small margin over two hundred thousand dollars.

HISTORY OF THE NEW NATIONAL THEATER. 93

And as the eye gaze roves around, taking in all the details of beauty, style and comfort, we can surely afford to congratulate the liberal owner of the theater, who presents to the citizens of the country a theater which is not only a thing of pride to the Washington citizens, but also an ornament to the Capital of the mightiest nation on the globe.

MR. W. H. RAPLEY, MANAGER.

Mr. W. H. Rapley, who is now the sole manager of the National Theater, is in the prime of manhood, being twenty-eight years of age. He was born in the District, and educated first at Hanover in Germany, and then, on his return to this country, he was appointed to a cadetship at West Point. After a residence at the Military Academy for two years, he came to the conclusion that there was not a sufficient fortune for an officer of the army in time of peace, so he resigned, and returning here assumed the management of his father's stove business. For five years he was also treasurer of the Theater, and last year assumed the management of the house, associating with him Mr. Sam'l G. Kinsley, who had long been the business manager for the former lessee.

Mr. Rapley possesses a splendid physique, being over six feet in height, hansomely proportioned, and weighing about 220 lbs. He has a frank, manly countenance, and is justly popular on account of his obliging nature and affable temperament. He inherited much of his father's business sagacity, and is fully conversant with all the details of theatrical management. A successful managerial career may be predicted for him.

WHERE THE THEATER STANDS.

The site of the National Theater of the present day is simply unrivalled; there is no spot of ground in Washington that contains such varied advantages as this favored temple of histronic art, situated close enough to attract the multitude that throng Pennsylvania avenue, yet far enough off to be away from the surging crowds that often jam the streets. It is the very center of the city proper; surrounded by the business crafts and commerce on one arc, and by the fashion and money on the other half of the circle, it attracts alike the sturdy artizan, as well as the "average man" with no occupation in life except to cut coupons off of his bonds. It is within walking distance of all the high grade hotels; it is the confluence of several lines of horse cars, that either pass the door, or a few steps away from the main track in the avenue that connect with every line in the District, and ribbons the streets with its steel rails, and thus citizens from the most remote parts of the city can reach their homes after the performance without trouble or delay. The street where the theater stands that unites with Pennsylvania avenue at 14th street, some fifty yards from the National, seems to have been laid out especially for a theater, as there is but little traffic in this side street, and it is a most fitting place for the waiting equipages in the night time, free from any wagons, omnibusses, or herdics, who take the public avenue in preference.

The reason why the National is so popular with the people of Washington is patent to all who think for a moment on the subject. It is a link that binds the Washingtonians to the dramatic past. It is the oldest place of amusement in the city. The greatest artists of the world have trod its boards. It is historic, and a temple without traditions, lacks its greatest charm. It was a place that the forefathers of the present generation went when they were young, and they have handed down many kindly sentiments and oral reports of the palmy time when the old and new world sent its most brilliant talent to the Nation's Capital. There is no great actor of the modern era whose name is not inseparably connected with the National Theater; and so it is that the public love the immortal part of it, the soul as it were, that survives and hallows the spot, even though the body is burned, a fairer structure arises and opens wide its doors to an appreciative public. It may not be the same boards, the same stage, the same house, where Forrest, Cushman, Booth—the kings and queen of the divine art held the people in speechless awe, or boisterous joy—but the one spot on earth is the same, and neither fire nor water can obliterate it nor erase its glorious memories. It is historic ground, sacred to the memory of Thalia, Terpsichore and Melpomene.

The National Theater, either in its old form or in a new one, will endure as long as Washington is a Capital. Like the great arena of the Seven Hill'd City, it will at future ages be a relic of the Nations greatness.

TIMES CHANGES.

Fifty years is not long in the history of a city or a theater, yet what a difference in the New National from the first building erected in 1835. They had lamps then for light. Gas did not come until years later, and, says Scotch Bettie Cameron in speaking of it: "If it's not enchantment, it's much like it. In place of being fashed with wicks, you just turn a bit of spiggot thing and out spouts a light, like sour milk out of a barrel. I wish them muckle luck o' it, but it will be awhile afore my gude man catches me darning his stocking wi' a witch taper at chimney lug."

What would Miss Betta say about the electric light?

The theater habitue of 1835 would open his eyes in speechless wonder, could he see the revolving scenery of to-day, and witness the arrival of the train and departure of the steamboat; while one of the spectacular plays would make him voiceless from its magnificence.

M'LLE RHEA.

Though a Frenchwoman, Madamoiselle has spent several years in America, and in a measure we have adopted her. Certainly she will find nowhere in the wide world more sincere friends and loyal admirers than in this country.

A brilliant genius enclosed in an adorable fair, as Sylvia says:

Is she not passing fair.

Rhea, as "Juliet," is lovely; she has the sweetness of the violet, the purity of the lily and the grace and tenderness of a child. Her acting is natural—never stilted; and the human emotions are prelined by her genius and trained art, with the same fidelity that the camera portrays a scene or landscape. In her tender roles she appears probably at her best—

Each look, each motion waked
A new born grace.

THE GREAT FUTURE.

The stage is just inside the charmed portals whose key is talent, genius and labor. And never in the annals of the stage are such princely guerdons held out to those who dare to pass it. In no other profession of life is recompense and requital so liberal as the dramatic art gives to its votaries. The demand for good actors far exceed the supply; and millions of people are ready to welcome the true artist with all the encouragement and aid within their power. The dramatic instinct is inherent in man. The love of good acting is a part of his being, and now that the higher civilization has recognized the actor as the peer of the greatest man on earth, and the art of portraying the passions of humanity as the most elegant and refined of all others, so the being who is gifted by God with these traits, will find fame and fortune, and let us hope happiness, before the footlights.

In the coming theater, whose curtain is rolled up to night for the first time, what a history now in the womb of time, is before it. On these boards who is destined to play upon men—

From the lowest note to the top of the compass.

Perchance a supe—or soubrette—who knows? Like Kean he may now sleep on a doorstep for lack of wherewithal to pay his lodging. Like Neilson she may be wandering about the streets crying with hunger. And the New National will be the spot where her transcendent genius will blaze out in all its dazzleing splendor.

> Here come all unknown the girl,
> To incarnate the muse,
> To wear the mantle Rachael left,
> And walk in Siddons' shoes.

HISTORY OF THE NEW NATIONAL THEATER. 97

NEW NATIONAL THEATER.

SAMUEL G. KINSLEY...BUSINESS MANAGER

Monday Evening, October 5th, 1885, for one week only.
The Distinguished Emotional Actress,

R H E A

And her Unrivalled Company, under the management of Mr. J. W. Morrissey, will appear in a grand production of the new Romantic Comedy-drama by Barron and Bates, authors of " A Moral Crime," entitled,

LADY ASHLEY.

Produced with NEW AND MAGNIFICENT SCENERY, SUPERB STAGE EFFECTS, GORGEOUS COSTUMES, and the following DISTRIBUTION of CHARACTERS:

```
LADY ASHLEY........................................................RHEA
Lady Norman..............................................Miss Ella Wren
Margaret Vernon.........................................Miss Mae Clark
Mrs. Walters............................................Miss Julia Wheeler
Martha.................................................Miss Annie Mackay
Lord Neil Norman........................................Mr. A. H. Forrest
Major Drummond..........................................Mr. J. T. Sullivan
Jacob...................................................Mr. R. G. Wilson
Dr. Surgie..............................................Mr C. T. Vincent
Hudson..................................................Mr. Boyd Putman
Marcellus...............................................Mr. Percy Sage
```

ACT I.—Facination.
      ACT II.—Adoration.
            ACT III.—Revelation.
                  ACT IV.—Expiration.

Business Manager...J. W. McKinney
Stage Manager..A. C. Hilsdorf

THE ARGUMENT.

Margaret Vernon, by the death of an uncle, falls heir to Ashley Manor, a vast possession in England. The terms of the will provided that if the son of Sir Robert Ashley, who was sent to India at an early age, died unmarried and childless, Margaret, a niece of Sir Robert, would become the legal heir. Charles, the son, died in India as a bachelor, and Margaret was installed as mistress of Ashley Hall. By her acts of charity and benevolence, by her self-abnegation and good will toward the poor, and through her sweet and amiable nature, she endears herself to all with whom she comes in contact. Lady Norman, a wealthy neighbor, becomes her bosom friend. Her son, Lord Neil Norman, a young man of artistic and literary attainments, is a frequent visitor to Ashley Manor. Margaret falls desperately but silently in love with him, which is not returned by Neil, though by his gentle attentions, she is led to believe him not indifferent to her. Mr. Hudson, the family lawyer, appears upon the scene, and conveys to Margaret the painful news that her Cousin Charles did marry in India, and left a widow and child, who at that moment were in the village. Although overwhelmed by the intelligence, Margaret accepts the issue with womanly dignity and spirit, and invites the new heirs to Ashley Manor. Lady Ashley now enters, and after formal preliminaries, takes possession of the estate, at the same time imploring Margaret to remain and continue her duty of supervision. Margaret consents, after a struggle with herself, solely because by remaining she will still be near Lord Neil. At this crisis, Neil enters, his eye meets that of Lady Ashley, and they both become transfixed with a passionate adoration of each other, which, later on, develops into the most uncompromising love. While Margaret feels keenly her position, she still remains at the manor, because the love her people bear her will not permit her to depart. When the happiness of Lord Neil and Lady Ashley is at its height, a Major Drummond arrives from India. At his appearance Lady Ashley turns deadly pale and swoons. While in this condition, Major Drummond denounces her as an imposter—that she was not the woman who married Charles, for she was a governess in his Indian bungalow, and was still in India with her child, in ignorance of the death of Sir Robert. The deception on the part of Lady Ashley so conflicts with Lord Norman's high sense of honor, that he casts her off. Writhing under the humilation of her shame, and conscious of the loss of her lover, Lady Ashley loses her reason, and gradually becomes a maniac, and dies in Neil's arms.

ADDRESS

AT THE

OPENING OF THE NEW NATIONAL THEATER.

WASHINGTON, D. C.,

Monday Evening, October 5, 1885.

Written by EDWARD CRAPSEY.

Spoken by Miss JULIA WHEELER.

Here where only a few brief weeks ago,
Disaster came with fierce and lurd glow,
With cruel hand its ruthless torch applied,
And Havoc feasted as the Muses sighed,
Behold a Phœnix from the ashes come!
Behold the drama's new and splendid home!
Aladdin's palace, in a single night,
Arose to prove the Genii's wondrous might:
A summer's eve sufficed the nimble Gnomes,
To shelter fairies in palatial homes.
Our builders, chary equally of days,
Present this palace to admiring gaze.
While yet the waste of ashes scarce was cold
They have wrought marvels, as did wizards old;
So swift, so sure has been their wondrous skill,
So strong has Fate been held to do their will,
That here, to-night, in this resplendent fane,
The smiling Muses are "At Home" again.

Now it were well to heed the glories past,
Cull rich memories from a storehouse vast,
See how the Drama, Servant of fair Truth,
Has solaced age, and safely guided youth;
In ancient Greece, in grandest days of Rome,
Conserving morals, purifying home.
Then came Eclipse—through ages drear and long,

HISTORY OF THE NEW NATIONAL THEATER. 99

Gone was the Drama, hushed the voice of song;
Wrapt in such darkness that it could be felt.
Man at the strange shrines of dumb idols knelt;
Gone were the glories of the ancient days,
Homer and Virgil no more sang their lays;
Plato unknown, Bethlehem's star not come,
The world in gloom was Superstition's home.
When anxious man had long sought light in vain,
As the parched meadows yearn for fruiting rain;
When light came, and the Star of Promise rose,
To shine as the sun from the Zenith glows,
First born of hope, the Drama came to serve
With tireless brain, stout heart, and lasting nerve,
Man's full advancement to the highest plane;
To raise him from depths where had dormant lain
His better self—to place him without stain
Where all the sowing yields not chaff, but grain.
Shakespeare to fair Faith, and to Hope gave voice,
Bade all mankind in truer life rejoice;
Taught how from prompting of the heart within
One touch of nature makes the whole world kin;
Portrayed all passions, but was Virtue's Slave
With scorn's sharp lash pursued each arrant knave;
Created worlds as real as this of ours,
Came to earth as April's frequent showers;
Forcing seeds dormant into fragrant bloom,
With light serene dispelling winter's gloom.
As beams of morning rend the shroud of night,
Thus did he show the drama's magic might;
Thus from the mind took off a numbing pall;
Thus led a groping race from out all thrall,
Was faithful to weal of both church and state,
Made Vice on Virtue obedient wait.

Now here beneath this new and spacious dome,
Nestles the drama in its splendid home,
Here will its lessons in the coming years,
Move throngs to laughter, or compel to tears;
Here will the key notes of all passions sweep.
As the wild winds the bosom of the deep.
Here be bond maiden to eternal truth,
Here be safe beacon to the tempted youth;
Here surely guide us in the pleasant path
That leads aside from sin, and shame, and wrath;
Here modest purity on all entail;
Here kindly hush misfortune's croning wail,
Here drawn the poison from sin's serpent tooth;
Here uphold Charity, and Love, and Truth,
Here do the work that God gives man to do;

Cast down the false, ever uphold the true;
Here purify, and here make bright, and clean,
As a fair river with its shimmering sheen.

Here paint all Nice in colors to repel,
Here with the virtues in full concord dwell;
Here grey griefs throttle and all joys enhance,
Here with quick fancy's quaint conceits entrance;
Here give to dust that "is a little gilt"
Satires bright blade, and blade unto the hilt,
Here always "aim at folly as it flies,"
Here build for wrong a lasting Bridge of Sighs;
Here faithful mirror hold to nature up,
Here take the bitter dregs from sorrow's cup;
Here budding childhood and old age delight,
Here give fair visions to expectant sight.

This is our task—this we shall strive to do—
Offer our patrons all that's bright and new;
No laggards, we, biding behind our day,
To vex the night with some trite, worthless play.
What in the new is good here will be found,
Yet sometimes will we roam familiar ground.
Our aim be always to instruct, delight,
To lead from darkness into blithesome light.
Bidding hearty welcome to this vast throng,
With drama bright, and subtle charm of song,
We promise pleasures always royal cheer
To all who are, or ever may be, here.

BUILDERS AND CONTRACTORS.

A. B. MULLETT........................Architect for the Front
J. B. McELFATRICK & SONS, of N. Y. & St. Louis, Architect for the Theater,
SAMUEL S. HUNT.............................Superintendent
GADE & MEYER..............Contractors for Brick Work
CHILDS & SONS...................................Bricks
J. VEIHMEYER....................................Stone
E. N. GRAY & Co..................................Iron
GEO. A. SHEHAN.................................Lumber
DAN'L SMITH & SON ....Sash, Doors and Blinds
W. E. SPAULDING & Co............................Painting
A. A. PRAELL.............Wood Carver Interior Decoration
MME. M. E. BINGAMAN................Drapery for Boxes
L. BAESSELL & SON.............................Frescoing
JOS. THOMAS..................Stairs and Lobby Finish
EMMICK & QUARTLEY.....................Lobby Decorators

C. B. Demorest.. Chairs
Jas. Lockhead................... Plumbing and Steam-Fitting
Cassidy & Son..Gas Fixtures
Smith, Bridge & Co. ....Electric Appliances
Whittier & Co............................Boilers and Elevator
Henry E. Hoyt..Drop Curtain
Chalmers-Spence Co ....Asbestos Fire Proof Curtain
J. F. Manning & Co...Tiles
McLaughling & Co....................Concrete and Pavement
White & Overman................Galvanized Iron Cornices
Miquel Aleo...Mirrors
Julius Lansburgh..Carpets
Cheeney & Hewlitt........................Interior Iron work
Einbigler & Adler....................Brass and Nickle work
L. H. Schneider & Sons.................................Hardware
John Humphrey..................Superintendent of Plasterers

ROSTER OF OFFICIALS.

The full Roster of officials and employes both in front of the house and behind the curtain, is as follows:

W. H. Rapley ....Sole Manager
Samuel G. Kinsley..........................Business Manager
Chas. A. Shaw ....Ticket Agent
Hank Schlosberg ....Messenger
Chris Arth ....Leader of Orchestra
W. H. Romaine ....Main Doorkeeper
James Jamison ....Dress Circle Doorkeeper
John Riordan.............................. Gallery Doorkeeper
R. E. Vennerman...............................Special Officer

USHERS.

James Craerin,   Walter Bradford,
J. Barratt Spaulding,   A. B. Griffith,
Zeff Schlosberg,   Henry Wallace.

Henry A. Sauter ....Master Machinist
John G. Buss.......................................Scenic Artist
John E. Williams.......................Master of Properties
Walter Lockhead,..............................Gas Engineer
Alfred Specht...............Master of Supernumeraries
Albert Johnson...Engineer
Margaret Russell......................................Janitress

www.ingramcontent.com/pod-product-compliance
Lightning Source LLC
Chambersburg PA
CBHW020157170426
43199CB00010B/1073